CRASH
AND
BURN

Rising Through The Ashes
After The Real Estate Collapse

KEN SARNA

ISBN: 1482523876

ISBN 13:   9781482523874

Library of Congress Control Number: 2013902943
CreateSpace Independent Publishing Platform
North Charleston, South Carolina

DEDICATION

This book is dedicated to all of the homeowners and real estate professionals who have trusted my firm to address their underwater mortgage problems. Without their trust in us I could have never gained the experience that is needed to form the opinions outlined within this book or been able to help so many homeowners.

Table of Contents

Introduction

I have always been someone who likes helping people and addressing the difficult problems that many others choose to avoid. Based on that and the fact that the real estate collapse has impacted my life in many ways I decided to write a book outlining the current problems we are facing and what is happening in the trenches to correct these problems. It has taken me two years to complete this book as I found myself constantly trying to update certain items as things have changed, but also due to the fact that there are so many different variables that needed to be addressed. I have broken down the numerous factors that led us into the current real estate crisis here in the United States. Understanding what investors and banks are doing to help get through this crisis is extremely important if indeed we are going to grasp what is really going on. We need to acknowledge the mistakes that were made and try to find solutions in order to not only get through the current issues, but also ensure this type of collapse never happens again.

I want to give you a little background on myself as well as my company so you will understand exactly what my experience is and how I have acquired my current knowledge base and the perspectives portrayed in these pages. I am not a long-term real estate agent, nor am I an attorney claiming to know everything. I am someone in the trenches dealing with the banks on a daily basis and have been since 2008. I come from a business background, having graduated from Creighton University in 2001.

After graduating I moved back to my hometown of Las Vegas, Nevada, which is now the epicenter for underwater properties. During the boom I worked as a mortgage banker putting together mortgage loans throughout the country. When the local market began to collapse, the owner of the mortgage bank I worked at asked if I wanted to help on a project he was putting together. Between the uncertainty in the market and wanting to help my friend, I agreed to participate without knowing exactly what I was getting into. We were liquidating toxic mortgage portfolios for a variety of investment groups that actually owned these distressed and overleveraged mortgages. These investment groups were smart enough to realize that the situation was not showing any signs of recovery and they were not comfortable sitting on these portfolios and allowing the market to collapse while they had no way to accurately forecast potential losses. Rather than waiting to see what was going to happen, they decided to be proactive in getting rid of the toxic mortgages as soon as possible in a variety of creative ways. In doing so they actually reduced their total losses significantly. If they had not acted when they did, they would have allowed home values to depreciate further, thereby losing even more money.

After working on the project for a while, I saw numerous changes taking place within the company and decided to change my path. I felt that I could help more people by opening my own company and using that same approach while working on behalf of homeowners against the banks. I opened The Millennium Consulting Group, Inc. in Las Vegas, Nevada. We are a licensed mortgage negotiation firm that has negotiated loan modifications, short payoff refinances, settlements of second/third liens and short sales. We have successfully closed thousands of transactions over the last few years, helping homeowners address their specific problems while maintaining a conversion rate of nearly 90 percent.

With so many successes, we have familiarized ourselves with the various programs that have come out at the different banks and servicing companies. Understanding these programs enables us to educate homeowners on all of their options and explain which ones make the most sense based on each of their unique situations. In doing so, we help put each of these homeowners in the position to decide how to address the problem in a way that will put them in the best financial position in the future. It also positions my firm to successfully process and negotiate transactions with the numerous banks to either make it financially logical for each homeowner to retain the property or figure out the best exit strategy for our clients.

Within this book I will briefly break down some of the causes of the real estate boom we experienced from 2003 through 2007 and then the unimaginable collapse that inevitably followed. The boom could not have happened at that level without numerous factors all falling into place. Some of the key players that contributed to create the perfect storm for this unprecedented real estate boom were the banks, lenders, real estate professionals, developers, investors and homeowners/speculators.

I will be outlining the different home retention programs used early in the collapse by what I refer to as the "smart money" as well as the programs that were introduced once the larger banks finally started to grasp how bad the problem truly was. I will be discussing the main foreclosure alternative homeowners and banks are currently pursuing and the hurdles that get in the way of getting to the desired outcome. Each option has certain benefits, depending on the individual predicament a homeowner may be in, so I will explain the benefits of each to give you a better understanding of them.

In my opinion the sooner each underwater homeowner decides what option is best for him/her and addresses the problem, the sooner we will be able to stabilize these communities and start on the path toward recovery. Once everyone can work jointly to get through the current crisis, we will then need to rebuild confidence in the minds of future home buyers that homeownership is still part of the American dream.

CHAPTER 1

The Real Estate Boom

When discussing the real estate boom, I want to be clear that I am considering not one single market but numerous markets that saw home prices soar at unbelievable rates. Not every market experienced dramatic appreciation during the boom, but the markets that did have suffered in the subsequent years. Generally the most booming markets were warm-weather cities being driven by baby boomers on the verge of retirement age.

Since I am from Las Vegas, I will use that specific market as an example of a market that has warm weather, numerous entertainment possibilities and prior to the boom, had extremely low home prices. Las Vegas was one of the most booming markets, along with parts of Florida, Arizona and California. Homeowners and investors alike saw these areas as a great opportunity to invest in a desirable market with possibilities of high returns. The potentially huge upside along with low purchase prices was extremely attractive for real estate speculators all over the world.

In most markets, appreciation from 1980 to 2002 was fairly consistent at 2 to 4 percent a year. After 2002 as the boom started, the rate of appreciation jumped up to historical double-digit highs. These dramatic increases could not have happened without numerous factors paving the way. (See Graph 1)

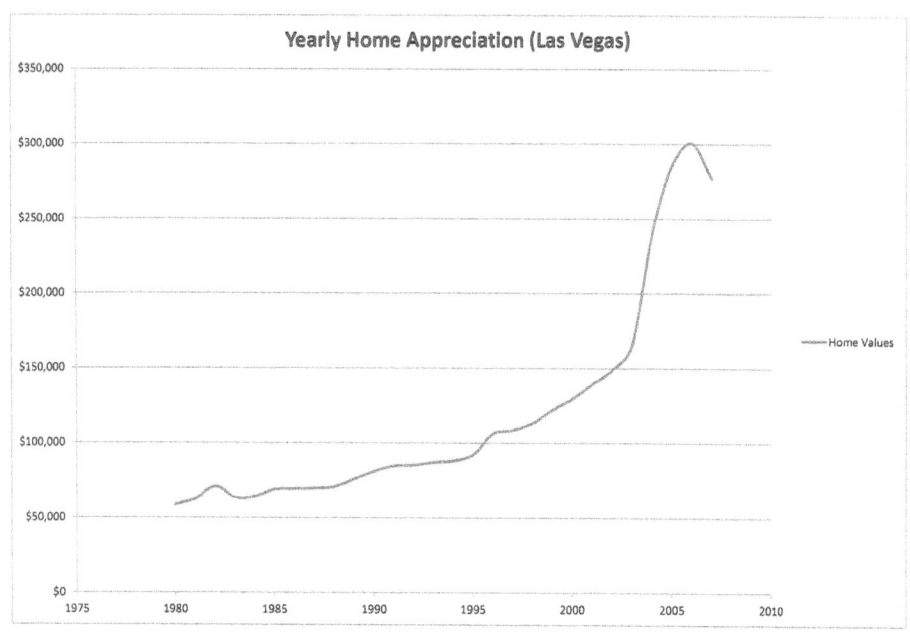

Graph 1

When I purchased my first home back in early 2003 in Las Vegas, I remember it being a big decision. I wanted to make sure I was getting the best home I could comfortably afford. I went to a mortgage broker to run my credit, see how much I would need as a down payment, and get an estimate of what my monthly payment would be on a particular property. After meeting with the lender, I expected to be putting down 10 percent and my monthly payment was going to be roughly $1,600. I felt comfortable with the numbers and decided this was going to be the house I would purchase. I put an earnest money deposit down on the home while I waited for it to be built. It was a 2,100 square foot home, and the purchase price was $205,000 with the selected upgrades. I expected it to be about six to eight months before I could move into my new home and I had hopes that the purchase would be a solid long term investment based on historical trends.

During the months of construction, I saw numerous changes in the market. Every time I went back to the builder to check the status of my home, I noticed that the base price for the same model had jumped $8,000 to $15,000. I was obviously happy to see this but also thought it was strange to see prices adjusting so rapidly. During one of my visits to the property, the sales agent I was working with told me they were going to lock out investors soon. If I wanted to purchase another home at the current price, I needed to act fast. I thought about it and in the end felt more comfortable only purchasing the one home, as I did not want to take on an additional cash down payment or the monthly financial obligation of another property.

As I got closer to actually closing on my property, a coworker of mine referred me to a different lender so that I could get a secondary opinion. I was not opposed to getting a second opinion, so I set up a meeting to see what they could offer. This lender told me I could actually put no money down and finance the whole amount needed to purchase the property. Why fork over a large down payment when I could finance the whole amount and my monthly payment would only jump about $180? I ended up going with the new lender and financing one hundred percent of the purchase price. It had only been seven months, and the property had already increased in value from $205,000 all the way up to $265,000.

I use this example to demonstrate how quickly these home values were increasing and how easy it was for a home buyer or speculator to form certain conclusions, such as the following:

- If I buy a home, it will increase in value significantly to the point where I can make tens of thousands of dollars in a short time frame.
- I had better buy a home now because if I don't, I may never be able to afford one in the future as the prices continue to increase.
- If I buy multiple homes now, I can make as much money as possible in the shortest amount of time when I flip them.

I also wanted to demonstrate how quickly lending changed and how banks were getting much more aggressive in order to get people into mortgages. I didn't even have to verify my income. All I had to do was show the lender my bank statements and a solid credit history. Numerous other factors clearly aided the boom, but lending was a critical piece of the puzzle. Just in the few months I waited for my home to be built, I went from needing a 10 percent down payment and verifying all my income and assets to putting no money down and verifying only my assets.

This adjustment in lending guidelines, along with the other changes to come, was a huge aid to the boom. Without this adjustment, speculators and nonqualified buyers would have never been able to get into these homes we now see being foreclosed upon at historical rates throughout the country. If you can put no money down and get a property showing a trend of appreciating 10 percent-plus a year, how could you not fall into the trap of buying more properties than you could truly afford? Or, in another case, how could you not buy a home before you were truly ready when you were concerned that the prices would continue to increase to the point where you would not be able to afford one in the future?

Mortgage/Lending Changes

After purchasing my first home I went to work for a mortgage bank where I familiarized myself with what it takes to qualify for a home loan. This was also at the beginning of the boom we have all heard about and many of us became victims. The word was spreading rapidly that buying a home in certain areas was a sure home-run investment and would be a quick way to make huge returns. People who would have never been comfortable buying a home and taking on that financial responsibility were now jumping in, becoming homeowners, and, in many cases, purchasing multiple properties. Feeling confident they could find a way to make the payments in the short term, they felt they would be set up for a big pay day after two years, when they would be awarded the full appreciation amount tax free.

The rule is that after you have occupied the property for two years, you can sell it and avoid the capital gains tax that would be associated with the payout. During this time I also saw loan programs adjusting even more, going from the full doc loans of the past, where we had to verify income, assets, and credit history, to the stated income loans, where all we verified was credit history and assets. A buyer could simply say he/she made a certain amount of money, and that number was used in getting the loan approved, as opposed to verifying their true income through pay stubs as in the past.

The banks then got even more aggressive and came out with the stated income / stated assets program, which allowed buyers to simply state how much money they made and how much money they had in the bank. Neither would ever be verified. All that was required was a solid credit history and that the buyer was currently employed. Both the income and assets were estimated by the applicant/buyer or the loan officer and could fluctuate dramatically. Lenders along with the buyers, generally inflated these numbers to show much more income than what was really being generated by the borrower, and lenders rarely knew how much money the buyer truly had in the bank.

As if these new loose programs were not enough, the banks then came out with new loan programs that verified even less than these initial programs did. Appreciation was happening at such a rapid pace that the banks felt they were not going to have any exposure, and, if indeed the homeowner did default on payments, the bank would be able to foreclose on the property and could capitalize on the appreciation themselves. Hence the no-ratio loan and no-doc loan programs were released.

No-ratio loans were loans that only verified assets; the total debt ratios were not taken into consideration. When I say debt ratios, I mean the debt-to-income ratios commonly associated with verifying that a person has the ability to repay the loan. The two debt ratios that have always been used are the total debt ratio and the housing ratio. Total debt ratio takes the borrower's current monthly obligations (credit cards, auto loans, student loans, mortgages) and uses it against the gross monthly income of the borrower. The housing ratio (monthly obligations associated with the new loan they are trying to obtain) takes into consideration the new expenses that would be associated with the new purchase. These expenses would include the monthly loan payment, property taxes for the property they were buying, any home owner association fees associated with the home being purchased and the insurance coverage for the home. Both ratios have been historically used to ensure that the buyer has the ability to afford the payments, not only on the new purchase but also based on other financial obligations the buyer already had.

The new and aggressive no-ratio loan allowed investors to purchase multiple homes and avoid issues with getting their loans approved. The no-doc loan actually allowed buyers to purchase a home without verifying anything but their credit history. Clearly these loan programs aided all the speculators and investors in getting multiple properties while enabling them to avoid being required to use their personal funds for a large down payment. In essence these buyers were getting into properties with the expectation of high returns, all while putting none of their own money at risk if indeed the market did start to slip. With no skin in the game, buyers are obviously more likely to walk from the property if and when things start to adjust for the worst.

After all these programs made it that much easier for a speculator or investor to get overleveraged buying real estate, the new problem banks had in trying to get more people approved for more loans was handling the negative cash flow issue on investment properties. If an investor had a mortgage of $2,000 a month and the rental rates in that area were only $1,400 a month, then covering the negative each month without putting his or her own money at risk was impossible. This issue could have stalled the purchase ability of these overly aggressive speculators, but then the banks came out with another even more aggressive loan program. In an attempt to help allow these buyers to get even more overleveraged and buy more homes, they came out with the option ARM (Adjustable Rate Mortgage). The option portion of this loan is what makes this loan so interesting and the reason it is now considered the most predatory loan ever offered. The homeowner would now have four payment options to choose from every month:

1. They could pay the highest payment option based on a standard fifteen-year fixed PITI loan (Principal, Interest, Taxes, and Insurance).
2. The next highest option would be a standard thirty-year mortgage PITI.

The other two options enabled them to reduce their monthly payment significantly. These options were:

3. The interest-only payment (where the payment is reduced based on only paying the interest portion of the loan and cutting out the additional expense associated with paying the principal portion)
4. The new and very aggressive negative amortization payment. The negative amortization option reduced the payment significantly by cutting out another part of the payment and, rather

than investors coming out of pocket with their own money to cover the difference from what they could get from rental income, that difference would be added to the principal balance owed on the loan. In essence what this did was allow the homeowner or speculator to reduce the negative cash flow every month that would have been an out-of-pocket cost for them in the past. These homeowners and speculators assumed that the rate of appreciation would outweigh the additional amount being tacked onto the balance of the loan, which would put them in position to still capitalize when they sold the property for a huge profit. This loan allowed already overleveraged people to get back into the market and start buying real estate again with minimal personal financial risk.

How did the option ARM loan gain popularity? During the boom the economy was great with people generating sizable incomes in all kinds of professions. Some of these professions were not paying what they had historically, but, with the amount money being thrown around, these professionals were making much more than what they had been accustomed to. Numerous people got into the mortgage business with expectations of easily making large incomes during the boom. They were able to essentially be their own bosses and set their own schedule, while making large commissions.

I think the freedom to do what you want when you want was one of the main driving forces to the huge increase in licensed lenders throughout the country. I can also say that in the majority of cases, these were not highly educated and ambitious people, but rather they were the lazy people who wanted to take what was at the time, the easy road. Most were not looking to build a business of long-term success through hard work and honesty, but instead were trying to make a quick buck and that is exactly what they did during the boom. They got people into loans that may not have been in the best interest of their clients but in turn paid them the highest commissions. The option ARM not only enabled speculators to get more properties but also happened to be the loan that paid out the highest commissions to these loan officers, which is precisely the reason this loan was pushed so hard on the consumer by these less-than-reputable loan officers.

Investment Groups

When looking at the boom, we can not only look at the single transaction scenarios but must also take into consideration the larger pieces of the puzzle. Some of these include the investor pools of buyers that were coming together and buying large numbers of properties within a short time frame. These investment groups were a huge driving force during the boom.

Investment groups formed all over the country. The spearheads of these groups were usually real estate professionals who strategically aligned themselves with teams of people who were all looking for the same quick returns. These teams would usually consist of real estate agents and mortgage lenders who also received commissions from each transaction. The basic idea was to get people from all over the world to take a look at the appreciation rates and the potential returns they could get if they invested in these markets. As a realtor, why would you want to sell one property when you could sell numerous properties all at the same time? The basic idea of these investment groups was always pretty similar, but each was structured a little differently.

Remember that during the boom, the number of licensed real estate agents soared just like the number of licensed mortgage brokers did. It seemed as if every bartender, valet attendant and cocktail waitress in Las Vegas was also working on the side in one of these two industries. In most cases, these were not highly educated people driven to build a successful business long term but were more the less educated people driven again by the idea of being their own bosses, making their own schedules, and capitalizing on large commissions without needing to do all that much work. Homes that went on the market were selling in a matter of hours during the boom in these highly appreciating areas and that reality made it that much easier for someone to get into the real estate business without proper training.

Investment Groups with Legitimate Buyers

The more legitimate investment groups were targeting investors they could sell on the appreciation rates in certain areas and justify an extremely low-risk, high-return investment opportunity to. They would get as many potential buyers as possible to come to Las Vegas for seminars and show them how they could invest fairly little capital into a property located in a highly appreciating area and have very little risk on the investment.

The investment groups would demonstrate how they could cut the monthly expenses for these potential investors by renting out the said investment property, offsetting most—if not all—of the mortgage payments. Additionally, the investment groups would show potential buyers how they could then also take advantage of some of the lending programs that would enable them to put down a minimal down payment. Buyers could in most cases finance 100 percent of the purchase price and get the seller, who was generally selling the home for significantly more than they owed and therefore walking with a large amount of money at the closing table, to actually pay the buyers' transaction costs for them.

Every group or individual investor had a different expected hold time before they would then put the property back on the market and sell it in order to capitalize on the expected high appreciation. These groups with legitimate buyers were not always bad, as the buyers generally had the capital to cover the negative mortgage payments on a monthly basis.

The realtors involved with these types of investor groups would normally show and market their own listings, thus doubling their commissions. By double ending the transaction, they would work both the buyer and seller side of the deal and ultimately generate the commission from both sides. In most cases they would not even put properties on the MLS (Multiple Listing Service is the platform used by real estate agents to market an available property) as a property available to all potential buyers. Rather than open properties up to be viewed by all real estate agents and buyers in the area, they would instead hold them internally as pocket listings to market the property only to the buyers they controlled. This would ensure that they worked both ends of the transaction and that they made the most money at the end of the day.

In cases where the agent did not have a pocket listing that would enable them to "double end" the transaction, they would sell properties with certain builders/developers that they knew were willing to pay a much higher commission, enabling them to again accomplish the goal of making the most money possible on each transaction, which seemed to be the main driving force during the boom. The real estate agents who received the commission for the purchase would also be the ones listing the property for sale when they went back onto the market to be resold for the initial investor who purchased them. This again allowed them to make yet another commission on the deal and helped maximize their personal return. As you can see, these agents were reaping many benefits during the boom through these investor pools in the form of generating multiple commissions.

Investment group spearheads were typically more knowledgeable about the different loan programs and what it took to get these investors qualified, which enabled them to manipulate the system to a certain extent. In some cases they would pad different bank accounts with all the money to show enough to qualify for loan programs that only verified assets and then use the one bank account to buy multiple homes at the same time. They would also pressure the lenders into closing on certain days so they could buy multiple homes as primary residences in order to get the best loan terms possible. By purchasing a home as a primary residence, the buyer would capitalize on a lower interest rate that was unavailable with an investment property.

In some cases the lenders were all different and had no idea what was going on, but in others the lenders were aware and were knowingly structuring the loans in this manner. Both the leaders of the investment group and the preferred lender in most cases would sell the buyer on the option ARM, which generated the highest commission to the lender when it closed. At the end of the day, during the boom, the only thing that mattered to far to many real estate agents and loan officers was making the most money they could while doing the least amount of work.

During the boom I was invited to do a seminar with investors due to the normal lender being unexpectedly unable to attend. It was a last minute thing, but I thought it was going to be a great opportunity to build my clientele. Unaware of the sales pitch put together by the group prior to my being introduced, I started answering questions geared toward lending. Quickly the group began pushing the option ARM loan on these buyers due to the fact it minimized their monthly payments. I told them exactly what I thought about the different options available to them and explained what negative amortization really was. I always felt that the option ARM was an overused, misunderstood program with numerous risks. When I started expressing this opinion to the attendees, the leaders of the investment group made it clear that they believed this loan program was the best program available for the investors. They wanted me to talk about nothing but the positive financial upside of having the lowest payment and be optimistic that the trend of significant appreciation was going to continue forever.

They clearly had different objectives than I did going in and they were not happy that I voiced my opinion on this loan. Obviously, I was not asked to participate in other seminars held by this investment group and did not get many clients from the seminar I did attend. I ended up getting one client out of the seminar, and of course this couple wanted the option ARM loan. I tried to talk them out of it, but, at the end of the day, that was the direction they felt the most comfortable going in. They were a very nice couple with the same expectation as everyone else: that appreciation was going to continue. They were investing their savings in real estate and were actually coming out of pocket with a significant down payment. This ended up being the only option ARM I ever closed as a mortgage banker.

As these groups recruited more people to attend the seminars, they progressively got more aggressive and started transitioning into different, even more creative models. They started using straw buyers and equity-stripping schemes to make it even less risky for someone to purchase a home. By using these techniques, they were able to actually get carrying capital from the seller, which could help offset any monthly costs while owning the home. These costs include any expenses associated with owning the home that were not being covered by the rental payments that were being generated. It all goes back to what these people were willing to do in order to make a quick buck, regardless of the long-term consequences.

Investment Groups with Straw Buyers

When these investment groups realized they had already used up most of the legitimate buyers and were not internally capitalizing on the appreciation themselves, they had to come up with more ways to close on transactions but also get involved in the returns when the initial investor then sold the property. In order to attract a different type of buyer, these investment groups got creative and started offering new opportunities to a different kind of investor—the straw buyer.

They started to offer money to individuals who had the ability to get qualified for a mortgage while only offering a fixed return. The straw buyer never had any interest in home ownership or managing the property but was simply agreeing to be the buyer of record for a fixed return. The investment group would maintain, manage, and cover the mortgage on the property until it was resold. The idea was that if they could get a straw buyer who wanted nothing to do with buying a home but liked the idea of making a quick $5,000 to $10,000 just to sign some papers, then the investment group (realtors) could capitalize on the large commissions at the time of the purchase and again when the property was resold.

This model enabled the investment groups' spearheads to again make even more money because they also capitalized on the appreciation when the property was resold. In the minds of the people putting together the investment for the straw buyer, this was a way they could internally generate the most money—all while risking the least. They felt there was no down side as long as the appreciation continued, so would the big pay days.

Equity Stripping

What I mean by equity stripping is purchasing the property not at its listed price but actually inflating the purchase price based on how much the real estate agent or mortgage lender could get the appraisal to come in at. If they get the appraisal to come in higher, then they could use that additional capital to carry the investment, pay off a straw buyer, or carry the costs of the investment. The agent(s) involved would have the seller give them the cash back for the difference of the actual listed price and the current inflated appraised value of the property, which would be used as the final purchase price. These equity-stripping models were used with legitimate buyers as well as straw buyers. During the boom it did not matter what method was used, as most people only cared about how much money they were making. Equity stripping was just another way to creatively avoid taking the risk of actually putting any skin in the game.

Appreciation was happening at staggering rates, and it seemed that everyone assumed it would never end. The next problem these investment groups encountered was the need to get additional upfront capital to carry the investment. They countered that problem by offering the seller a higher price than what they were asking and then getting the seller to give them the difference back in cash. This enabled them to offset the mortgage payments and carrying costs while waiting to resell for a big profit. It also aided in getting higher comps for properties in the area, which artificially inflated values even more than they already were. Most sellers during the boom could care less, as they were still getting what they wanted when they sold the property and in many cases were exempt from the income taxes associated with the sale. (If the property was owner occupied for two of the last five years, then the gain was not taxable.)

In order to get the capital to cover the negative, they would structure these transactions similar to the outline below:

Property's current listing price on the MLS: $200,000

Amount buyer with inflated appraisal would offer: $220,000

The buyer and their realtor would then make sure the appraisal came in high enough for the buyer to get the loan and then have the seller give them back $20,000 after the property closed escrow.

Cash back to the buyer / investment group: $20,000

This money was commonly split between the investment group and the individual who signed the purchase contract as the straw buyer. In this situation, the realtor who put the investor or straw buyer in place would get the commission of $6,600 (3 percent of the purchase price) if they only worked the buyer side of the transaction. As explained earlier, the norm during the boom was that they would only submit offers on properties when they were also representing the seller. As a result, they would get $13,200 (6 percent of the purchase price) in commissions along with a piece of the cash distributed back from the seller to the buyer. Once again it all goes back to making the quick buck and many real estate agents were just as guilty as the lenders, if not more so, as in these cases.

Once the transaction closed and the investment spearheads got the commissions, along with the additional capital from the seller, the actual buyer of record may not have any financial responsibility to make the payments or manage the property. The investment group would then take on the full responsibility for renting the property and covering the negative cash flow—until they could be the ones who capitalized on the big return when they resold the property. Even though the buyer of record qualified to purchase the property and signed the loan documents, in many cases they had no real interest in home ownership. Most of them only wanted the quick return promised by the investment group.

The above examples of equity stripping and straw buyers are two common ways that many investment groups leveraged themselves as much as possible, while putting next to nothing into the deal. They used straw-buyer schemes and equity-stripping techniques to take advantage of the system in attempt to generate thousands of dollars for themselves. As shown in the above example, the buyer was typically sold on the fact that they would get a quick return. These buyers never thought that the investment group would not honor their part of the deal, as they knew that their interest was in reselling the property and getting the big return. The problem was that if the appreciation did not continue, what would happen then? Most of the players never thought of that as a possibility, as real estate was expected to always continue to appreciate—or at least that was what people thought during the boom.

I am not trying to single out the investment groups here in this chapter. Numerous other factors also contributed to the boom. I feel that many of the investment groups helped bring a high number of buyers to the market and used numerous schemes to help people better understand how to overleverage themselves. The reality is that developers and builders did exactly the same things in an attempt to sell as many homes as possible, also enabling them to capitalize on the real estate boom. They never took the long-term consequences of these actions into consideration. Most of the people involved only cared about making a quick buck as home prices continued to soar.

Home Builders / Developers

Home builders and developers contributed to the real estate boom in a variety of ways. Prior to the real estate boom, it was customary for real estate agents to get 6 percent commissions on each transaction. They would split the commissions evenly at 3 percent to both the buyer's agent and the seller's agent. During the boom, some of the developers and builders started offering significantly higher commissions to real estate agents who brought buyers to the table. This made it even more attractive for real estate agents to push their clients toward buying from specific developers/builders. It all goes back to the realtors trying to make the quick buck, and these developers knew exactly what they were doing. By dangling the carrot for these realtors, developers knew this would increase their chances of getting more buyers to their developments and ultimately help them get rid of their inventory.

Some of the builders also used equity-stripping techniques, like the investment groups did, to ensure the values on future closings would not be an issue. I have heard of certain appraisers working alongside builders and actually using homes that were still in the process of being built as comparables to validate the high purchase prices of other homes they were trying to close. The home prices were increasing so rapidly that finding buyers was easy. However, they could not justify the high prices through an appraisal, which was an issue for buyers when trying to get the needed financing to close.

As if offering increased commissions to realtors was not enough, the next problem builders encountered was ensuring that the appraisals were coming in high enough to justify the higher values. They even went so far as allowing buyers to change their contracts after the home was built in order to give the money back to the buyers in cash (similar to what was going on with the investment groups, mentioned earlier). An example of this follows:

Buyer locks in a purchase price of $215,000.

After the home is built, the builder gives the buyer the option to close at either the initial contract price or the current appraised value of $245,000.

Transaction closes at $245,000, and the buyer gets cash back in the amount of $30,000.

Why would the builders do this? Well, many of the builders were more than happy to do this because it gave them the ability to use the closing price to help justify increased prices on other homes getting ready to close. Without these recent comparable sales at the higher dollar amount, they would have had issues getting the other properties to appraise at the necessary value. This took place regularly to enable the builders to unload their inventory and avoid appraisal issues down the road, all while capitalizing on the highest possible returns. In order to ensure the buyer could get the needed financing and that the appraisal would come in at the needed price, these builders resorted to these tactics or other aggressive ways to keep values up.

As things began slowing down, some of these builders/developers started offering very aggressive incentives to buyers. Some actually offered to pay the mortgage for the buyer during the first three to twelve months of ownership. In many situations, a homeowner could actually purchase a home with no money down during this time and have no mortgage payments for an extended period after moving in. This made it that much more attractive, regardless of the purchase price or the buyer's ability to repay the mortgage, for a person to purchase a home they truly could not afford.

It got to the point where getting into a home was all that mattered. No longer was a builder building a quality home or a buyer being particular about getting exactly what they wanted long term. It became more about getting the home quickly so they could make huge returns while the values continued to soar. As a builder, the quality of the work took a backseat to getting the home completed as quickly as possible, regardless of what corners needed to be cut. This combination made for the perfect storm. The builder could make their money and homeowners could care less, as they only intended to sell their homes quickly instead of keeping them long term, as in the past.

Developers of condo conversions were also commonly using these techniques, as well as others, to get rid of inventory. A condo conversion was basically an apartment converted to a condo so it could be sold for high profits during the boom. Some developers offered huge commissions to realtors who would sell their properties. I have heard of several such conversions in Florida where the developer was offering commissions plus bonuses to anyone bringing in a buyer. Developers would also offer buyers huge cash-back incentives, making this type of investment was very appealing on the surface. The problem with this was that when buyers got one hundred percent financing and didn't have any skin in the game, then they were handed $20,000-plus in cash at closing. Many of them defaulted on the loans shortly thereafter. If they did not go into default, that many of these condos were put back on the market to be sold, which then caused an oversaturation of homes on the market, thus causing values to decline.

This was primarily taking place between 2005 and 2009. During that time a friend of mine came to me asking my opinion on buying an investment property in Florida. He was thinking about buying a condo and the developer was going to make the first twelve months of mortgage payments for him. The developer would then give him back a significant amount of cash when the transaction closed—$30,000. I told him I felt it was a very risky deal and shared my numerous concerns. If the developer was giving him money back, was that allowed and properly disclosed to the bank giving him the loan? Also, if the developer was selling these units in this manner, what was going to happen after a year, when all these investors had to make payments? I would think that would have caused all of them to be for sale, which would reduce values through oversaturation; otherwise they would all be in default, which would also work against him by reducing the values significantly.

He ultimately backed out of the deal, but this shows how aggressive and greedy these builders/developers were getting. They were trying to close on as many transactions as possible, regardless of the long-term risks or manner in which they closed. During the boom, it simply didn't matter as long as they were making money.

Each of these factors identifies a different cause of the real estate boom we've all heard about. These factors are also a significant piece of what started the problem to begin with and eventually led to the real estate crash that we are all still dealing with today.

CHAPTER 2

The Real Estate Collapse

A s discussed in chapter 1, the years during the real estate boom were great with a thriving economy and extremely low unemployment. People were making more money than they were accustomed to making and then putting it back into the market, which kept the boom alive. All of that was about to change as home values stopped increasing at such rapid rates in 2008 and actually started decreasing. No longer were homeowners trying to sell their houses at the right time to get the best return. Instead, the more savvy homeowners/investors started scrambling to unload properties as quickly as possible. Some were still optimistic that values would come back and decided to wait it out— never expecting what was about to happen. (See Graph 2)

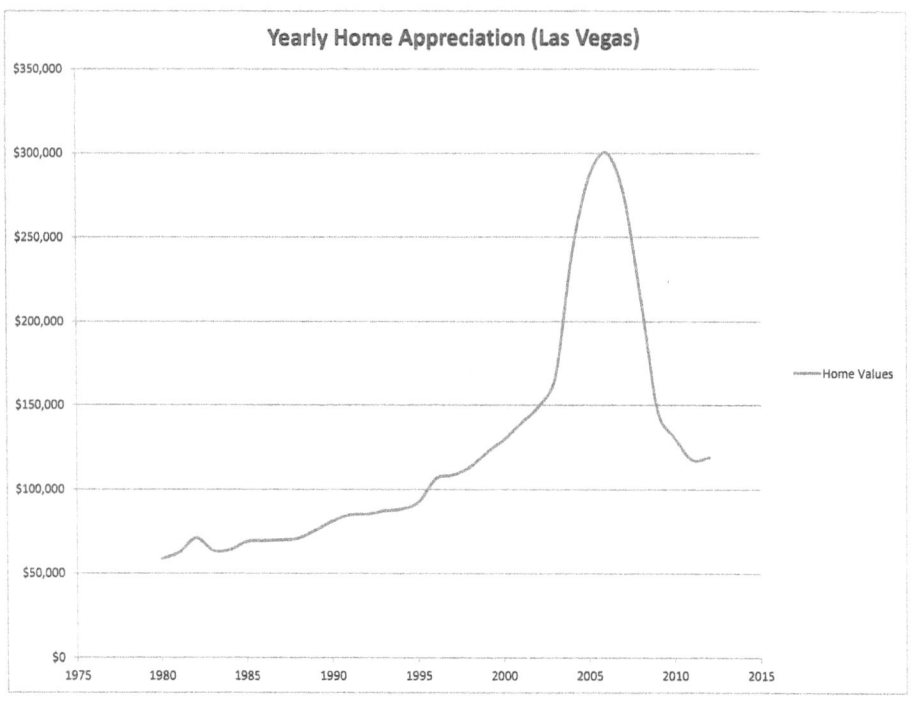

Graph 2

The economy was changing and unemployment rates started increasing, which made it that much more difficult for many homeowners to cover all their expenses. As home values continued to deteriorate and the available inventory of homes increased, homeowners had to decide how to deal with the problem in these highly depreciating markets. But, to a certain extent, that decision was made for them. They could either allow the property to bleed them to death financially over time or look at other exit strategies. Other viable options for them would be trying to get a loan modification, allowing the property to go into foreclosure, filing for a bankruptcy, or trying to do the right thing by short selling the property. These were all negative options, but in a situation this bad, there are no positive outcomes on the horizon. No matter how much money you make, or even if you have the ability to make the payment, the reality is that no reasonable, hardworking person wants to throw it away on an investment that has gone bad. I understand the emotional ties people have when it comes to their homes, but homeownership has always been a long-term investment—and now that investment had gone in entirely the wrong direction. At the end of the day, it comes down to making a financial/business decision in the best interest of your family long term.

Below is an example situation outlining the average homeowner's scenario in Las Vegas:

Purchased the home in 2007 for	**$380,000**

Financed 100 percent of the purchase price with two loans:

<u>**First Mortgage Balance**</u>	**$304,000**
First Mortgage Payment (Monthly Interest Only)	**$1,488**
Property Taxes (Monthly)	**$160**
Homeowners Insurance	**$50**
Monthly Payment	<u>**$1,698**</u>
<u>**Second Mortgage Balance**</u>	**$76,000**
Second Mortgage Payment	<u>**$364**</u>
Total Monthly Payment	<u>*$2,062*</u>
<u>**Home Value in 2012**</u>	<u>**$145,000**</u>

Think about the above situation, which is truly the norm in some of these highly depreciating markets, and the reality of what homeowners are facing in those markets. What would you do if you found yourself owing $380,000 on a home that had a current market value of $145,000 and was still depreciating? On top of that, you are making interest-only payments, so your $2,062 a month is not putting even a dent in the principal balance you currently owe on the home. This is your reality, all while your neighbors (who just purchased the same or a similar property in the last few months) are paying $930 a month and only owe $140,000. The breakeven point on this investment is fifteen-plus years down the road. That is if indeed we start seeing home values appreciate at a modest 2 to 4 percent a year and that was not happening.

I think it is awful that hardworking Americans, who have found themselves in this unfortunate situation, are being stigmatized for going into default on their mortgages when the banks are forcing them to do exactly that. Many businesses, including these same banks, builders, and developers, who paved the way for the boom, have found themselves in a financial crunch today. These businesses make decisions based on minimizing losses for stockholders or executives of the companies, and these decisions are made regardless of the companies' ability to make the payments. When they default on debt in order to cut costs, they are not looked down upon and in many cases are seen to be making a smart strategic decision based on long-term profitability for the company. Even if they have the capital needed to continue paying on the debts, at the end of the day, their responsibility is minimizing losses, cutting costs, and ensuring they secure the best long-term returns.

I feel that homeowners caught in this situation are also responsible for making that same long-term financial decision. The difference is that they are not doing it to please stockholders or company executives. These homeowners are doing it to put their families in a better financial position for the future. If the boom and monumental collapse that followed has taught us anything, it is that we never know what is truly around the corner and that we need to plan for the worst, as opposed to being optimistic that the market will recover and that home values will come back. Unless homeowners are willing to wait ten- to twenty-plus years for home values to come back, all while throwing money away on the property, they may want to take a minute to understand the severity of the problem and address it sooner rather than later.

Mortgage/Lending Changes

During the boom properties were selling quickly and people were getting home financing much easier than ever before, but this trend was about to change. As property values stopped increasing and loans began going into default, the banks made quick changes to reduce the risk they were taking on by approving these overly aggressive mortgage loans. It seemed to happen almost overnight staring in 2007. Certain loan programs were discontinued immediately. Even if the loan was previously approved and ready to close, banks were forcing the buyer to go back and re qualify for another loan program. If the buyer could not show that they truly had the ability to afford the payments, then they would not be able to get the loan they needed to buy the home.

The first loan program to be discontinued was the option ARM program, which was, in my opinion, the most toxic loan program ever released. The next loans to be discontinued were the no ratio and no doc programs, which were also seeing increasingly high default numbers. These changes were in my mind expected, as they had to tighten up and stop lending to anyone with a credit score over 560.

In the months following those initial changes, the default rates on loans continued to climb. Numerous factors led to these defaulting loans, but the main factor in my opinion was that these homeowners never had the ability to make the payments from the beginning. When the values were going up, these homeowners were willing to do anything to make the payment based on their hopes for a big payday when they turned around and sold the property. Now that the values had stopped going up, these homeowners were no longer willing to work two jobs to make the payments, as they no longer had any hopes of getting the high returns they initially expected. If you purchased a home you could not afford with the intention of selling it and making a quick return, how could you justify retaining the property without any hope of generating a return?

While time homeowners were losing hope for a big payday, home values continued to deteriorate and the demand to build more homes declined. The economy was also going in an entirely different direction. Unemployment numbers started to increase and people who had gotten a loan they could not truly afford were now trying to sell the property as soon as possible, causing an oversaturation of homes on the market and causing home values to drop even more significantly. Some of the loans going into default were also adjustable mortgages that were now adjusting in a way that increased payments even more than what the homeowner could already not afford. In certain markets people were overleveraged in real estate and, rather than being able to handle one mortgage, they were slowly depleting their savings in order to cover mortgages on numerous properties, which inevitably had to come to an end. This was the reality of what was happening, and the banks had to offset the risk associated with owning these mortgages in a hurry.

The banks then discontinued the stated income and stated asset programs tightening up loan guidelines even more. It seemed as if the mortgage business went back twenty years in regard to what they required from a buyer applying for a mortgage. After the boom, it was as though expecting the buyer to actually qualify for the loan was something unusual. I remember going to work and getting notified that every loan in my pipeline that was previously approved for closing now had numerous conditions to be cleared prior to moving forward or had to be completely resubmitted under a different loan program. Certain financing options being offered on Friday were no longer available on Monday, so I now had to explain to my clients that I needed to get additional documents from them. I had to explain that due to the market conditions, I needed to actually get their loans re approved for a different loan program even if they were previously approved. That was the last call I ever wanted to make, but it was completely out of my control. All I could do was work within the rules given to me by the banks—and in this case, those rules were changing rapidly.

Numerous clients were upset about delays or issues we were encountering, but the reality was that they did not understand the significance of the problem at the time. Early in the collapse, all clients still cared about was getting the property they wanted, even if they could not afford it, as they still had hopes of the market rebounding. As for those who ended up not closing on their loans and not getting the property they wanted, I think it was the best thing that could have happened for them. I hope they did not find another lender to get them a loan, and instead sat on the sidelines putting themselves in a position to purchase the same property today at half the price.

I would imagine most of them ended up going to other lenders who may have still had access to certain loan programs. While the lending changes were happening quickly, not all mortgage banks and brokers implemented them at the same time. In most cases, if another lender funded the loan for these clients, it may have actually put that mortgage company out of business, or at least led to them being forced to shut their doors. It would also have locked the homeowner into the new property, which inevitably would have depreciated to the point that they would find themselves in the situation of being underwater on the home significantly within six to twelve months.

With the number of mortgages going into default, numerous other loan requirements also tightened up. One of the most important changes had to do with appraisals. During the boom it seemed like you could get an appraisal to come in at the purchase price and the appraiser could always find a way to justify it. Now the appraisals were coming in lower and being scrutinized much more. This was a huge factor in what was about to take place over the next few years. No longer was an appraiser able to use homes still under construction as comparables to justify values; they had to use true sales within the last sixty to ninety days to validate true fair market value. Getting higher values based on market trends, as during the boom, was no longer possible since the trends were now depreciating, which also had to be taken into consideration when determining home values on these appraisals. No longer were properties getting purchased in a matter of hours. They were now sitting for months, along with numerous other homes for sale on the same street.

The oversaturation of these markets was also taken into consideration on appraisals. Banks were now ripping appraisals apart, only accepting appraisals from certain companies and limiting the distance the appraiser could go away from the subject property for actual comparables. By not allowing appraisers to go outside the immediate subject area to justify the value and making them use foreclosure sales and short sales as comparables, the banks were reducing their internal risk on new loans. They were also driving property values down by forcing appraisers to be much more conservative in their approach. Appraisals are now being put together in a way that will justify the real value, as opposed to during the boom when they were using the highest sales and trends to get the highest values possible. The banks wanted to reduce their risk, and the only way to do that was to make sure they were lending on properties for what they were truly worth.

They even took away the lenders' ability to communicate with the appraiser altogether to make sure the lender or real estate agents could not talk the values up to get the value where they wanted. Now the lenders had to order the appraisal from a third party, who sent the appraiser to complete the inspection. The third party does all the communication with the appraiser and is the direct contact to the appraiser if an issue arises. This new process also took away the equity-stripping techniques real estate agents used during the boom. No longer was it as easy to get an appraisal to come in exactly where they wanted it to be, so the capital of these investment groups was quickly running out.

Prior to the collapse, every market saw an increase in the number of mortgage banks and mortgage brokers that were opening. These mortgage companies were structured as either actual mortgage banks that would fund the loan at closing or mortgage brokers who were the third party that facilitated the loan out to the actual bank that funded the loan at closing. If you brokered the loan out to another party, then you did not have as much risk as when you actually banked the loan in house. Essentially, once you brokered the loan to the third party, you no longer had any real risk associated with that loan performing. If indeed you banked the loan, you would fund it internally but in most cases would turn around and sell it in the secondary market to an investor.

The majority of these mortgage banks did not hold loans internally and made money by selling them off to investors in the secondary market. They did have more exposure due to the fact that if they sold a loan to an investor, that loan had to perform for the investor for a certain time frame. If it did not perform or was not structured to meet their guidelines, then the mortgage bank who closed the loan would have to repurchase it back from the investor and could be stuck with it long term, or at least until they resold it to a different investor. This was something these mortgage banks wanted to avoid, as repurchasing a loan cost them money.

During the boom a seemingly endless number of investors would purchase large numbers of loans in the secondary market. Each investor would have certain guidelines, and if the loan met those guidelines, the investor would buy it in the secondary market with the expectation that they would make the long-term profit associated with holding the loan and getting the payments. As the boom turned to the collapse, these investors were no longer buying loans in the secondary market. They now tightened the criteria to the point that when a mortgage bank funded a loan and tried to sell it in the secondary market, they had no one interested in buying it. This forced the mortgage bank to hold the loan internally, which was not something they had ever intended to do.

As a result of the secondary market drying up, over 350 mortgage companies in the US went out of business between 2006 and 2009. I remember a website that focused on tracking ailing mortgage companies. As a lender I went to this site every few days and it seemed like every time I did another company was being added to the list. Both mortgage banks and brokers, ranging from smaller local operations all the way up to huge national firms, were being forced to shut down as a result of the collapse that followed the boom.

Home Builders / Developers

As the market adjusted and home values were not appreciating at the same ridiculous rates as in the past, builders and developers were caught in a unique situation. They could no longer manipulate home values, due to the appraisals being held to a higher standard. They had all their homes under contract at prices that they would never appraise at, and they needed to determine exactly how they were going to address this problem. If they forced the buyers to honor the contracts, they would never be able to obtain the needed financing at the contract prices, so some of the more reasonable builders and developers actually worked with the buyers and reduced the purchase prices to the current fair market values. That enabled the builders/developers to get rid of the standing inventory while at the same time showing their clients that they were willing to work with them, which in my opinion, was the right thing to do. Below is an example of how this worked:

<u>Contracted Purchase Price</u>	$350,000
<u>Buyers Earnest Money Deposit</u>	$8,000
<u>Home's Current Value (after eight months of building the property)</u>	$295,000

Builder agrees to reduce the contract price from $350,000 to $295,000 so the buyer can get the appraisal and still close on the property.

The builder did not get the expected return for the property in this situation, but they did get rid of the standing inventory and secured the highest possible price for the property, based on its true current value. If the builder took the current value as the purchase price, then they would not be risking anything if the market continued to deteriorate and would still make a profit on the transaction. This also showed good faith to the buyers and the builder/developer who took this approach should be commended.

Other developers and builders decided to go the exact opposite direction with how they addressed the issue. Instead of getting rid of the property for the true current market value, they decided to hold the buyer hostage at the contracted purchase price. If the buyer could not close, then the builder would keep their earnest money deposit ($8,000 in the above example) and then sell to another buyer for the current value. Obviously this was the wrong thing to do on numerous levels but goes with the basic premise of what got us to this point: only caring about the quick buck, regardless of the repercussions. These builders and developers decided that instead of working with the buyer based on the fair market value of the property, they would instead tell the buyer that they had to honor the contract and either find a way to come up with the nearly $50,000 difference to close on the purchase or forfeit their earnest money deposit.

This situation was unfortunately the scenario many buyers found themselves in, and the majority ended up walking away from the hard earned funds they used for the earnest money deposit. The above example uses a typical earnest money deposit, but some buyers actually had over $100,000 deposited on certain high-rise condos in Las Vegas and were put in the same situation. Can you believe this was actually happening and no one stepped in to help? As a result of the values dropping, hard-working people were losing their savings to these builders/developers who tried to force them to pay significantly more for a property than it was really worth. I don't know anyone who came up with the difference to close on the transaction, but I'm sure it happened. I feel bad for the people who found themselves in this predicament and even worse for those forced into bringing the additional funds to the table. They essentially threw that money into a fire and burned it without getting any benefit from it at all.

As for the builders and developers who took this approach they typically got what they deserved. They took the properties back after essentially stealing these buyers' deposits and then had to sit on the standing inventory while the values continued to plummet. The more the values deteriorated, the more these builders and developers lost as a result of their malicious approach to the problem. Instead of doing the right thing, they tried to hold buyers' money hostage, which forced many of these builders and developers into bankruptcy. They defaulted on their debts when they knew they were not going to be in a position to capitalize on the huge returns they initially expected.

The builders/developers of condo conversions and high-rise condo projects that were hot purchases during the boom were now doing the same thing within their developments. The difference was that they typically required a much more significant earnest money deposit, which meant that these buyers ended up losing much more than just a few thousand dollars. No longer could the developers sell buyers on getting money back at closing or paying the payments for the first year. At this point, the values had dropped so significantly that most of these developers shut down the developments and took any money they were able to capitalize on during the boom. This obviously left the unfortunate buyers who did close with high mortgages on properties that were worth significantly less than what they owed. It also left them owning a property that was in complete turmoil because the developer was no longer around to complete it or to be held accountable for the numerous construction defects left behind.

Investment Groups

Investment groups who were selling homes in a matter of hours during the boom now saw homes sitting on the market for weeks and even months with no interest from buyers. This was extremely evident early in the collapse within the high-rise-condo and condo-conversion markets. These same developments had offered higher commissions in order to entice real estate agents to sell the product. Almost overnight the secondary market purchasing these mortgage bundles completely dried up, and no one was willing to buy loans issued on condominiums, specifically these high rises and the condo conversions. I expect the banks noticed a significant rise in the number of people defaulting on those particular mortgages, and that forced them to pull back quickly.

In order to get any interest from potential buyers, the owners of these properties and their agents had to slash prices significantly. That price reduction meant the seller most likely had to short sale the unit and that the agent was not going to make the commission he/she initially expected.

This reality also meant that the agent, if willing to work for a lesser commission, would also have to navigate the tedious short sale approval process, and that is not something most agents understood or were willing to tackle.

The difference to the agents' commission was due to the value of these properties declining so much. In order to get the larger commissions of the past, all they had to do was get the property under contract and wait for the buyer's funding to come through. Now if they wanted to generate a commission they would need to get a buyer and then process and negotiate the terms of the transaction in order to get the banks approval and ensure the seller would agree to the bank's terms within a short sale. Otherwise they could get paid $0, even after working the file for months. The value change of these types of properties in the example below is not normal in most markets but is the average here in Las Vegas.

Expected resale price during the boom:	$385,000
Commission at that price:	$11,550
Current resale price after the collapse:	$145,000
Commission at that price:	$4,350

As the boom came to an end and it became clear that properties were not going to appreciate moving forward, these investment groups obviously could no longer entice buyers with hopes of high returns. They were, however, stuck with the properties and arrangements they had already gotten into with their investors. How could they get these people out of the situation they had gotten them into? Unfortunately, there was nothing they could do. They were all stuck in these horrible mortgages and unfortunate circumstances. The option ARM loans were based on having a certain equity position, and now investors no longer had the required equity that had given them the lowest payment option every month. No longer could they make that low negative amortization payment that gave them the ability to add it back into the principal balance owed.

Now they didn't have any equity in their property and these investors who had taken advantage of this program with hopes of a small payment saw their required monthly payment doubling to one they could not afford. With the increased payments, they were all forced to tap into their personal savings or look for an exit strategy. In most cases they looked for an exit strategy quickly, but some of these investors did everything in their power to make the payments, even when it forced them to deplete their savings and liquidate their retirement accounts. Even with the changes in the market, some people tried to do the right thing and allowed a negative-equity property to bleed them to death financially before they came to terms with the harsh reality that selling the bad investment was truly the only way to go.

The straw buyers were the most victimized. The investment groups who promised to make the payments and cover the expenses associated with the property now realized that the investment was never going to pay out and stopped making the payments. In some cases they even stopped talking to these straw buyers altogether, leaving them to deal with what was going on by themselves. These investors who initially wanted nothing to do with the property but wanted the quick return they were promised were now being forced to deal with tenants on their own and were also stuck making the payments themselves, if indeed they wanted to maintain a solid credit history.

The same realtors who got straw buyers into these properties and received the high commissions were now not honoring the initial agreements and were even disappearing altogether. Why honor these agreements when they knew they didn't have any money to make? Any reasonable real estate agent would discuss the issue with the client and decide on the best exit strategy, which likely would have been a short sale. These realtors could have helped their clients get out of the bad predicaments they were in and they could have earned another commission at the same time. The commission would not be the big payday they had initially anticipated and it would have taken a lot more work going through the short sale approval process, but in the end, they could have helped to correct the bad situation they helped create.

The problem was that short sales take a lot of work, and these realtors who were only motivated by the quick high return had no idea how to facilitate a short sale or the desire to deal with those types of tedious transactions. These agents only wanted the big payout and were willing to honor the initial agreement as long as that hope was still alive. When they lost hope for the high return, they had no reason to continue paying the mortgage or handling the rental of these properties. Most of these agents left clients to deal with the problem on their own and abandoned them altogether. This left these straw buyers without any direction on how to deal with the problem, their personal credit at risk due to the fact that the investment groups were not paying the mortgage, and without any idea how to manage an investment property.

Unfortunately other investors were also adversely affected by the collapse due to the leveraging tactics being used during the boom. The buyers who used equity-stripping techniques during the boom now found themselves in a terrible situation. They had not only paid top dollar for the property but had actually paid more than it was ever truly worth. They increased the price when they purchased the property and then took the money to cover the carrying costs associated with the investment. These carrying costs were pretty high and the capital was running out fast. As the money ran out, values were deteriorating quickly and the hopes they initially had of getting a big payout were gone.

Suppose you are the buyer. You now have no money left to carry the investment and the property is worth 50 to 70 percent of the mortgage balance. What option do you really have at this point? There aren't any attractive options and you will be forced to either take the credit hit by addressing the problem or accept the fact that you are going to throw money away on the property indefinitely until you can hopefully at some point break even, however many years it may take. In order to avoid losing more money, a homeowner can miss payments in attempt to see about getting a modification, move forward with a short sale, or allow the property to go into foreclosure. None of these options are very attractive, but in this type of situation there are really no attractive options. At the end of the day homeowners will take the credit hit associated with an exit strategy as soon as possible so they can start to rebuild their credit after the fact. The sooner they get rid of the property, the sooner they can start the recovery process.

Smart money moves made early in the collapse

As the real estate boom came to a screeching halt and home values started to go into a declining trend, all the different banks and investment groups that owned these mortgages had a different approach to dealing with the issue. This was way before the government started coming out with any programs or the large banks knew what they were going to do. These smaller banks and investors buying loans in the secondary market identified the problem much quicker than the larger banks ever did. In many cases they were also very proactive in addressing the problem. Every group had a different business model, but at this point they all found themselves in the same horrible predicament. They had no way to know if and when a loan they owned was going to go into default, how much more the values of the properties would deteriorate, or whether the market would take a small dive and then recover fairly quickly or would suffer a huge collapse that it would never recover from. These banks and investors couldn't possibly forecast potential losses on these assets or even minimize potential losses without knowing the answers to these questions. There was no black and white way to address the problem because no one had a crystal ball telling them what was on the horizon.

They all had huge exposure as a result of home values dropping so significantly and they had to identify what to do in order to minimize their losses and/or put themselves in a position to accurately forecast potential losses they may have to take in the long term. I refer to the investment groups that actually owned these mortgages and took a very aggressive approach to dealing with the issue early on as "smart money." I would say that the percentage of investors who went in this direction is relatively small, but the investors that did outsmarted the others in a huge way.

Prior to the government coming out with modification programs, banks, private investment groups, and hedge funds were internally seeking an avenue to liquidate their toxic mortgage portfolios and avoid the large losses projected in the future. I am not saying the larger banks were not as intelligent, but, based on all the red tape they had to go through in order to make a decision, they could not act as quickly as the more savvy investment groups who had the ability to call the shots on their assets. What these investment groups were doing that was extremely aggressive is referred to as short pay refinances.

A short pay refinance is a program that enables a homeowner in a depreciating market to refinance out of their current loan and get a new loan based on the true current market value of the property and current loan programs that were still available. If the homeowner in these cases could qualify for a new loan that met current loan guidelines, then it was the best possible strategy for all parties. It would enable the homeowner to get rid of any unknown adjustments in the future and lock in a fixed-term mortgage while at the same time reducing the principal balance owed on the property to the home's current fair market value.

Why would a smart investment group do such a thing? The basis of this program was not only to help the homeowner. These investors who owned the loans were still driven to make money in the long term, which was exactly why they would participate in a program such as this. It enabled them to get rid of these toxic mortgage assets as soon as possible while getting rid of any future exposure that would come as a result of further deterioration of the market. The question should now be: why did more banks/investors not participate in this program as opposed to wasting time and money on modifications programs that have failed miserably?

Below is an example outlining the net benefit to a short pay refinance for the actual owners of these mortgages, as opposed to waiting for the homeowner to pursue a short sale or default on payments:

Scenario 1: Foreclosure

Current Loan Balance	$250,000
Current Market Value	$150,000
Net Value after Foreclosure	~$103,000

This is an estimate based on the expenses associated with the foreclosure process, fixing the property, maintaining the property, and then reselling the property to a new buyer. These costs will fluctuate depending on the situation but will always cost the foreclosing party the most money.

Scenario 2: Short Sale

Net Value after a Short Sale	~$125,000

This is also an estimate, but typically the costs associated with a short sale are much less than with a foreclosure. Property damages are less likely on a short sale, and you can avoid other costs associated with the foreclosure process. The additional transaction cost associated with reselling the property adds up but is still less than what a foreclosure would cost and has fewer variables.

Scenario 3: Short Pay Refinance

Net Value after a Short Pay Refinance $138,000

As you can see, the true net to the bank is increased by avoiding the foreclosure or pursuing a short sale. By doing a short pay refinance, they increase the net return—in some cases significantly. The bank would get the homeowner into a new loan and could also avoid the transaction costs associated with selling the property. They also avoid paying the real estate commissions and would get the highest amount based on the current appraised value. In the other situations, they may have gotten lowball offers that were much less than the true market value of the property, but with this program, everything is based on the actual appraisal. In this situation, when they reduced the principal balance of the loan, they would most likely also get the homeowner to contribute additional money—which could only increase the net return.

I think any reasonable homeowner with a job would be happy to throw in an additional $5,000 to $10,000 to the bank when the bank is reducing the principal balance owed on the loan. That contribution could only help reduce the losses taken on by the bank. Below is an example of how this would work:

Current Loan Balance $250,000

Current Market Value $150,000

The clients in this situation get reviewed and are approved for an FHA (Federal Housing Administration, low down payment mortgage) loan based on meeting all the current applicable loan guidelines. This means they can get a loan for 96.5 percent of the current value of the property. The bank would then send over a reduced payoff for $144,750 (96.5 percent of the appraised value). This would enable the homeowner to reduce their current loan balance to $144,750 and get into a new thirty-year fixed-rate mortgage. The homeowner can now also retain their home long term. What the bank gets is the maximum net return, which is roughly $138,000 after miscellaneous title fees associated with the refinance. They could also capitalize on any additional contributions the homeowner may be willing to pay to participate in the program. The investor who owns the loan would then get liquid in that amount and would be in position to not only take out the uncertainty of additional deterioration of the market but also to reinvest that money into something that would produce a better return. The investor would obviously have to accept losses now but would be in a position for a much better long-term return as a result. At the same time the investor would be getting out of the unknown risk associated with owning those toxic mortgages long term.

Not everyone qualified for this program, but for those who did, it was a win-win for all involved. If the large banks would have followed suit and worked a similar program specifically within the highly depreciating markets, we may have been able to reduce the severity of the collapse and helped thousands of homeowners retain their homes, as opposed to what has happened in the last few years. Instead the large banks sat back and tried to come up with other creative ways to manipulate programs that would offer an element of relief to the homeowner on the surface while really only truly benefiting them.

CHAPTER 3

Home Retention Programs

Government Modification Programs

A s it became increasingly evident that the real estate collapse was not slowing down but was instead forcing home values into a downward spiral (while homeowners started losing their homes to foreclosure), the government decided it would step in and help. On the surface the government wanted to come across as looking out for homeowners who had found themselves caught up in the mess, but the reality was that it was also looking out for the government entities that actually owned these mortgages.

The most prevalent government mortgage agencies are Fannie Mae and Freddie Mac. Since these government entities own the majority of mortgages behind the scenes, they also had the most exposure once the collapse began. In order to work with homeowners and also slow down the rate of foreclosures, the government came out with numerous programs supposedly designed to help the situation. These programs were also put together in ways to minimize the losses these government agencies would potentially be forced to absorb on these bad loans.

It took time, but eventually the government had to acknowledge how serious the problem really was. In owning these toxic assets, the government decided it needed to put together programs to portray to the public that they were trying to help homeowners. After learning more about the programs and the qualifying criteria you can decide for yourself if they were truly trying to help or just attempting to minimize the losses they would inevitably be taking. If indeed these programs truly were designed to help homeowners, they would have come out with them sooner and would have been much more aggressive. Instead the government slowly rolled out programs clearly designed to reduce the interest rate and the short-term monthly payment for homeowners while also increasing the returns to the bank by extending loan terms. It took them a very long time to come up with a program to help these struggling homeowners and it is baffling that this is all they could come up with. After receiving all those tax dollars, I would have thought that they would have been competent enough to put something more beneficial together that would have been more impactful for struggling homeowners.

The government has come out with numerous modification or refinance programs over the last few years, but none of them have benefited the amount of homeowners that was initially anticipated. I think these programs have, completely failed for a variety of reasons. These programs were geared toward normal markets throughout the country that had not depreciated as significantly as some of the harder-hit markets—like parts of Florida, Las Vegas, Phoenix, and numerous others throughout the country—and were not addressing the real problems in those markets. In these harder-hit markets, an interest rate reduction was nothing but a Band-Aid on a much larger problem. Based on the narrow qualifying criteria for these programs, the vast majority of homeowners (who had high hopes for assistance after all the media attention these programs received) were denied any assistance after months of jumping through all the hoops associated with being reviewed for the initial HAMP (Home Affordable Modification Program) program.

Some of the criteria to qualify for the HAMP government program are listed below. It is easy to see why no one seemed to qualify:

- **Loan must be on a primary residence.**
  If you live at a different address or the property was a vacation home or an investment property, you are denied.

- **Your current mortgage payment (principal, interest, property taxes, and hazard insurance) must be more than 31 percent of your gross household income.**

  If your gross household income can cover these household expenses, then you are denied regardless of the value of the property or any extenuating circumstances.

- **The bank or servicer that has your loan must participate with the program in order for you to qualify.**

  Banks are not required to participate with these programs, and, due to the high volume of required forms that need to be completed, as well as the default rate on approved HAMP modifications, many banks do not want to participate. If your bank does not participate in the program, then you are denied. In many cases the bank could still deny your loan modification based on their discretion even if you fell within the published criteria for the program.

- **If you have a second or third mortgage, those need to be addressed separately.**

  These liens are still on the property and will need to be addressed separately from the main loan modification.

- **If you have more than two months' worth of payments in your bank account, you could be denied.**

  This shows that you need to have already bled to death financially before they will assist you in reducing your payment or help you afford the property. I think this also clearly shows that the programs are not set up to help homeowners until they have already given the bank as much money as possibly.

- **If the current payment is more than 31 percent of your gross household income then you may qualify to reduce the payment to 31 percent of the household income.**

  This sometimes causes the bank representative to tell you that you are prequalified for the modification. But then, when you get offered an $80 a month payment reduction, you are upset and feel as if you wasted time and were misled. That is another problem with these programs. It seems as if they get the homeowners' hopes up all to come back with an offer that is not enough to justify agreeing to the terms of the modification, or they get denied altogether.

- **Modifications typically require the homeowner to make payments for a three-month trial period.**

  It is supposed to be three months, but the reality is that the trial payments are being dragged out to six-plus months with no permanent modification being approved. In many instances the homeowner is denied after making more payments, which is another reason for the complete failure of these programs. If the homeowners have paid an additional six months' worth of payments after being told they will get a modification and then are denied, they are obviously going to be upset. The banks get more money while pursuing a foreclosure behind the scenes the whole time, and the homeowner is completely caught off guard. This has routinely happened and left a bad taste in homeowners' mouths toward the banks and the government for misleading them with hopes of assistance. If the homeowners are not going to get approved, I think it is only fair they be told that from the beginning so they can look at other options rather than get hit with a denial and a foreclosure notice without any time to prepare.

In order to be reviewed for the HAMP modification, you need to submit numerous financial documents. The main piece being reviewed for an approval or denial is the calculation of monthly living expenses and gross monthly income. If your living expenses (which consist of mortgage payments, credit card payments, auto loan payments, utilities, food, and any other monthly reoccurring payments you may have) are more than what the bank feels you can handle with a reduced mortgage payment, then they will issue a denial. Homeowners are essentially being asked to prove that they can afford to pay a reduced payment from what they were currently required to pay. If those payments are not very high, then they may issue a denial based on the fact that your other obligations are so low you can handle the current mortgage payment. Does any of this really come across as if this program was designed to genuinely help homeowners who are not able to make their current mortgage payments or who don't want to lose their homes? I believe it was purposefully structured in such a way as to ensure that anyone could be denied for any one of a variety of reasons and no one could ever be accountable at the bank. How could anyone make a valid argument that this was structured to be efficient or to actually ensure that homeowners receive help?

The basic logic of the HAMP program was to reduce homeowners' monthly payments, therefore putting them in a position to make the payments moving forward. In most cases, these government programs were also extending the terms of the loan to ensure the banks always profited even after reducing the interest rate for the homeowner for a period of time.

HAMP was put together in a way that would portray the banks as helping homeowners who were struggling to make their payments. The program, if homeowners could qualify (based on the criteria noted above), would essentially help reduce homeowners' monthly payments by doing two basic things: the banks would reduce homeowners' interest rates based on their financial predicament and would extend the life of the homeowners' loan terms dragging repayment of the loan out further.

The problem with this program is the basic structure. Typically, the interest rate would be reduced to as low as 2 percent. They would then lock in the new rate for the first five years of the new modified loan. After year five, the interest rate would increase 1 percent (which would increase the payment), and after year six the rate would increase another 1 percent (which again would increase the monthly payment for the homeowner). After year seven, the interest rate would again increase, this time to the capped rate for the remainder of the loan. This capped rate was typically between 4 and 5.5 percent. The problem was that the bank had already capitalized on both the first few years of payments and the front-loaded interest customary on a mortgage loan. So they had already capitalized on that interest the homeowner had paid them, and now the bank was extending the terms of the loan again to a new thirty, forty, or in some cases even fifty-year loan. Whoever put this program together was clearly looking after the banks' returns much more than trying to help homeowners.

Below is an example situation where a government loan modification could be extremely beneficial:

Current Loan Balance	$250,000
Current Loan Payment (Principal and Interest) with a 6% Interest Rate	$1,499
Current Home Value	$230,000
Reduced Loan Payment at 2% Interest	$924

In the above situation, this government loan modification program works perfectly. The home is not significantly upside down, and the monthly payment has been reduced by nearly $600. That kind of a monthly savings would be a huge benefit to a homeowner who has found it difficult to cover the monthly expenses associated with owning the property, and that reduction should enable the homeowner to retain the property long term. In this situation and others like it where the property is only upside down a small amount, the homeowner could realistically expect to see the property value coming back in the next three to five years. This would be a tremendous help to the homeowner and would enable the government and banks to accomplish the goal of helping people, while at the same time only needing to address this property one time and minimizing any losses they might take as a result.

Below is the same example but now in the situation where a government loan modification would not necessarily work out to make retaining the home truly in the best interest of the homeowner:

Current Loan Balance	$250,000
Current Loan Payment (Principal and Interest) with a 6% Interest Rate	$1,499
Current Home Value	$150,000
Reduced Loan Payment at 2% Interest	$924

In this scenario, which is more consistent with the harder-hit markets, even with the same monthly savings, the homeowner has really just put a Band-Aid on a much larger problem. The real problem may be that the payment was more than what the homeowner could truly afford. However, if they were to accept the same modification, the problem of owing $100,000 more than the home is truly worth would never be addressed. That type of a negative-equity situation is not going to be recaptured in three to five years but would take ten-plus years of solid appreciation just to get back to even. Once again, I am not trying to be pessimistic, but the reality is that appreciation could not be expected to the extent needed—and that must be taken into consideration. If the government was truly trying to help homeowners, why wouldn't they allow an element of principal reductions in these scenarios?

Below is a breakdown of how that would look in terms of total cost to the consumer over the first ten years of agreeing to this modification:

Annual expenses associated with the mortgage (principal and interest):	$11,088.00
Multiplied by # of years:	10
Amount paid into the investment:	$110,880
Principal reduction through payments covering the first ten years:	~$57,564
Property value if we were to see 2% appreciation each year for the first ten years:	~$183,000

In this situation the home would be worth ~$183,000 after ten years with an annual appreciation rate of 2 percent. The loan balance would be roughly $192,436 ($250,000 - $57,564) after the principal had been paid down over that same ten-year period, so the homeowner would have just spent over $110,000 in order to still owe ~$10,000 more than the property is actually worth. I think that money could have been spent in a number of ways that would have been much more beneficial to the homeowners and their family. This is the same mind-set that most affluent homeowners have in these highly depreciating markets.

Remember that during those same ten years, the homeowners could have completed a short sale on the property, restored their credit, and put themselves in a position to purchase another home for what it was truly worth. On top of owing less on the new home and having a much lower payment, the homeowner would also be in a position to capitalize on any future appreciation that may take place, as opposed to relying on getting appreciation in order to just break even on the investment.

No one knows what the future will bring, but positioning yourself to capitalize on any future increases is much better than hoping for positive future adjustments to chase the goal of simply breaking even. By agreeing to this modification, the homeowner is still going to inevitably wake up at some point and seek an exit strategy rather than wait for the problem to fix itself. Over the past few years, even when homeowners get approved for modifications, they typically go back into default within six to nine months when they have a negative-equity situation, such as in the above example. When that happens the banks are again forced to address the same property over and over again, which costs them even more money.

Obviously these government programs have flaws, which is why loan modifications across the country have not been as effective as initially anticipated. Maybe the government will come out with new programs in the future that will enable more people to qualify and enable homeowners to feel as if it is a long-term fix—as opposed to a short-term Band-Aid. The reality is that no one is going to help fix the problem for you. Your bank is not going to call you out of the blue and reduce your principal down to the fair market value of your home, nor is the government going to come out with a permanent fix for everyone to bail you out. After seeing what has come out in the last few years, I have lost all hope of either of those things happening.

Instead we will continue to hear about new programs on the horizon that homeowners may qualify for, as long as they are current on their mortgage payments. This is ridiculous but it is what we continuously hear in the media. Again, it is a tactic giving homeowners false hopes while the bank still gets their money. At this point, most homeowners understand the significance of the problem and hopefully understand the need to look at their situation and choose how to address the problem individually so that everyone can move on toward a brighter future as a community.

Other Modifications

Most banks have now adopted internal modification programs that have different qualifying criteria than the government programs. Most are structured similar to the government programs but seem to be a little less strict with their guidelines and in some cases have more beneficial terms for the homeowner. The main questions to ask as a homeowner who is getting a modification are broken down below:

- Is the new interest rate fixed or will it adjust in the future?
- Is the new payment interest only or principal and interest?
- Does the new payment include the property taxes and hazard insurance, or are those going to be separate expenses?
- How many years are the new rate and payment going to be in place? Sometimes the lenders stretch these out to a new forty- or fifty-year term. If that is the case, you want to be aware of it.
- How much is owed on the property after the modification? Sometimes the lenders reduce the principal balance, increase the principal balance, add fees to the back end of the loan to be paid as a balloon payment or do a variety of other things. Homeowners always want to make sure they are clear on exactly what the terms are so that they can avoid surprises in the future.

A homeowner pursuing any type of loan modification should be aware of the different things the banks may try to slip into the terms that they may not want to agree to. The problem most banks and investors have with modifications, specifically in highly depreciating markets, is simple and justifiable: why would the bank want to spend the time and money needed for handling modification requests when they have seen the majority of approved modifications end up going delinquent within nine months anyway? If the homeowner (who gets approved for a modification) owes more than the property is currently worth, then at some point they are potentially going to step back and reassess the real problem. They may wake up at any time and decide that even though the bank did reduce the mortgage payment through a modification, they still have an issue based on the reality that they owe tens of thousands of dollars more than their home is worth. This is happening more often than not, especially in markets that have seen home values decline over 20 percent.

Because homeowners do go delinquent after being approved for modifications so often, banks have to take that into consideration when reviewing for loan modifications. This is why many banks flat out do not want to do modifications and would rather work with the homeowner on a short sale. Banks and the investors who actually own these assets have an unknown future liability associated with retaining loans on their balance sheets and modifying them. The last thing any of them want to do is spend money to help facilitate modifications and then have the same files come back again needing attention six or nine months down the road due to the homeowner going delinquent on the modified payment.

Most investors want to get the money back so they can re-invest it into something that will generate a better return. These investors should have been more aggressive in pursuing short pay refinances early in the collapse, which would have helped them accomplish this goal while at the same time would have helped get the homeowners into a position to retain their homes. Another issue banks and investors have with modifications is the reality that the economy is still on a downward trend. Unemployment numbers are still high, so if they modify a loan today there is no guarantee that the homeowner won't run into further hardships moving forward which would potentially put the same file back on the banks desk as a short sale or foreclosure anyway.

Principal Reductions

Principal reduction is talked about all the time. It is something that everyone wants to see happen on their personal loan, but, it is not happening in the majority of cases. Does it happen where a bank actually reduces how much the homeowner truly owes on their property? Absolutely, it does happen, but it is not happening as much as people would like to think.

When I was working to help liquidate mortgage portfolios for banks and investment groups, they were giving principal reductions to everyone in order to get rid of those toxic loans. That was how they decided to attack the problem internally on assets they controlled. These were not large banks, like Wells Fargo or Bank of America, and were not dealing with the number of loans and the red tape that those larger banks have to deal with. The larger banks have been much less willing to work with homeowners in granting true principal reduction. I have heard that these larger banks can't do principal reductions because they have to be fair across the board with all of their customers, but I don't necessarily find that to be a valid argument. Each situation is different, and since the actual bank only owns a small percentage of the mortgages, I don't believe they would have a hard time explaining that the investor who owns the mortgage is actually the one issuing the principal reduction and not the bank itself.

Think about it from a big-picture perspective. If these large banks only own ~13 percent of the loans they service the monthly payments on and the bank can acknowledge that they do not own the mortgage being reduced, then how can it really be that difficult? These investors need to acknowledge that they are in a losing situation and just cut their losses now so that we can all work through this horrible situation. Until we work through it, we are all going to suffer as a result of it dragging out much longer than needed.

Fannie Mae and Freddie Mac specifically need to stop fighting the issue and start allowing homeowners to get out of this bad debt so that they can move on with their lives. Instead these government entities (funded by our tax dollars) have plagued the situation even more by being unreasonable, inefficient, and difficult to deal with at every level when it comes to assisting the very tax payers that have bailed them out and allowed them to grow to this level. Why is it that Fannie Mae and Freddie Mac seem to have a pass when it comes to this problem? In any other business being mismanaged to this extent, it would be customary to see a complete overhaul of management as the current management has failed to execute on anything in the last five years. Or is it the servicers they have chosen to work with who are failing and passing it onto Fannie and Freddie? Is anyone accountable or will they both be allowed to constantly point at the others and say they are the problem?

Now that the main question everyone seems to ask has been addressed, let's look at the difference between a true principal reduction and a phenomenon that some people perceive as principal reduction but is not principal reduction at all. People come to me all the time and say they negotiated principal reduction on their mortgage. The reality is that in most cases, what people think is a principal reduction is actually principal curtailment. There is a big difference between the two, and if you look into it further you will see that your principal has not been reduced but instead has been pushed back and added to the back end of your loan. Below is an example of principal reduction and then principal curtailment, each based on the same scenario. The difference is typically not explained to the homeowner by the bank but is obvious if you really look at the paperwork.

True Principal Reduction

Current loan amount: $200,000

Current value of the home: $130,000

The lender agrees to reduce your loan to an amount they feel you will be able to handle moving forward, based on your income, and an amount they feel you will be happy with in order to ensure they do not have to come back down the road and readdress the loan in the future. At the same time, they want to make sure they are still profitable long term.

The bank or investor who owns your loan agrees to reduce the principal amount owed to:

$145,000

This means that you have new loan terms, which are typically fixed for a new thirty-year period at a fixed interest rate based on a new balance that is less than what was originally owed. There are no hidden terms. Even if you were to sell the property, you know that you owe $145,000 as opposed to the original $200,000. Certain banks/investors would do this in some cases, as it ensures they generate the best long-term revenue while also significantly reducing the probability of the homeowners going delinquent in the future. Even if the values deteriorate further, the homeowners will not be upside down so much that they cannot reasonably recover within a few years with appreciation, which will at some point happen.

Principal Curtailment

Current loan amount: $200,000

Current value of the home: $130,000

The lender agrees to modify your loan based on your *current* income. They can essentially make the payment affordable by reducing the loan amount that your payment is based upon. Instead of your monthly payment being based on a $200,000 loan at 6 percent ($1,199 a month, principal and interest) your new payment is based on a loan amount of $130,000 at the market rate of 4.25 percent ($640 a month, principal and interest). This new scenario seems to work out, and some homeowners fall for this as a way to retain a property they are emotionally attached to. The bad thing commonly overlooked is that in the small print of the modification agreement, it states that the $70,000 principal difference (i.e., $200K-$130K) is now being added to the back end of the loan and is still owed on the property. If you decide to sell the property, you still owe $200,000 and cannot sell it without it being a short sale or bringing in the money to cover the difference. If you do keep the property and pay off the current loan, that $70,000 difference will be owed as a balloon payment at the time the loan is supposedly paid off. This will force the homeowners to then take out a new loan to pay off the balloon portion, thereby putting them back into a position of still being required to pay off the full initial balance that was owed.

Principal curtailment was designed as a way for the bank to again be profitable in the long term by costing homeowners even more money in the end. Misleading homeowners with principal curtailment offers is almost as predatory as the loan programs the banks came out with during the boom, which put these same homeowners into this situation in the first place. These programs are not in the best interest of the homeowners and, should no longer be offered as a way to deceive homeowners who are upside down on their property. Banks should explain to homeowners the true terms of any modification they may be offered so they are clear about what they are dealing with rather than misleading homeowners.

Subordinate Lien Settlements

One of the more aggressive and truly helpful programs that some investment groups and banks are willing to work with homeowners on is settling junior liens that are on a property. A junior lien is a second mortgage (or third) that is behind the senior lien or first mortgage. These could be home equity lines of credit (HELOCs) or second mortgages that were customary through 80/20 loans where homeowners financed one hundred percent of the purchase price through two mortgages, and third liens are sometimes taken out to put in a pool or landscaping after a purchase. When a bank is willing to negotiate a junior lien settlement that enables a homeowner to reduce their overall debt on their home and also reduce their monthly expenses. In many situations this can be extremely helpful and actually put the homeowner into a position to retain a home that may have not been possible without the settlement being approved.

This is not something all banks are willing to do but it is something we have been able to get accomplished numerous times for our clients. In order to attempt this option, you would need to go through your banks specific process and nothing is ever guaranteed. Success in getting your bank to settle a subordinate lien can be a very beneficial outcome for all parties involved. This program is more prevalent in highly depreciating markets and may not be as prevalent in a stable market that has not deteriorated 20 percent or more. Below is an example situation demonstrating how this would work and why it is so beneficial:

Home was purchased for $350,000 and the homeowner secured a 100 percent loan through

-an 80% first mortgage and

-a 20% second mortgage

first mortgage balance: $280,000 ($1,678 a month payment, principal and interest at 6%)

second mortgage balance: $70,000 ($588 a month payment, principal and interest at 9.5%)

Home's current market value is now $260,000 (The first mortgage typically needs to be owed more than the property is currently worth in order to get the bank to agree to a settlement on a junior lien. Since the first mortgage is owed $260K and the home is only worth $240K.

Second mortgage settles the $70,000 junior lien for a flat $8,500 (The net requirement on a settlement would be dictated by the financial predicament of the homeowner and can typically be negotiated to between 5 and 15 percent of the current loan balance.)

Why would this be a viable option for all parties?

The junior lien holder (bank or investor who actually owns the mortgage)

Since the property is clearly overleveraged, the loan is already in a bad situation. If the homeowner decides to short sell the property, the most the senior lien holder (i.e., the owner of the mortgage) will typically allow to go toward the junior would be 3 to10 percent of the total loan balance—in this case, $2,100 to $7,000. This is if the homeowner tries to move in the direction of a short sale and if the senior lien holder agrees to the short sale, so it is not guaranteed that the junior will secure those funds. On top of the above not being guaranteed, it is also a much longer, more drawn-out process, which lengthens the amount of time it will take for the junior lien holder to actually get the money. If the homeowner decides to let the property go into foreclosure, then the senior will take everything received through the foreclosure and reselling of the property, leaving the junior lien holder with nothing.

It makes sense for second and third mortgage holders to settle out those debts and help homeowners get back to where it makes sense to retain their property and avoid the other options. It also enables the junior lien holders to get liquid quickly and maximize their net (i.e., their bottom line). Some homeowners have decided to flat out stop paying the junior liens and only pay their first mortgage. That leaves the junior lien holder in a position to either get nothing or escalate foreclosure—all to get nothing in return, as the money received in the foreclosure would pay the primary lien holder first prior to them getting any of the proceeds if there is any left. As opposed to getting nothing, it makes sense for junior lien holders to be proactive in working out a settlement with homeowners as soon as possible so they can both make the best of a bad situation.

The homeowner

Settling these subordinate liens could completely change the overall situation for a homeowner. In the scenario above, if the homeowner wants to retain their home and make it make sense to retain it, then a settlement of the junior lien would completely make sense. In this example, it could reduce the total debt on the property to the point where it is only underwater a small, manageable amount of $20,000 (the amount of negative equity based on owing the first mortgage $280K and the property only being worth $260K). That is something that could easily be rectified within a few years at a modest appreciation rate. It also enables the homeowner to reduce the total monthly expenses by $588 (the monthly payment of the junior lien in the example above), which is another benefit to a homeowner who may have taken an income reduction in the last few years due to the economy.

Qualifying for settlement of a junior lien is not guaranteed. Below are a few rules that typically come into play:

- The first mortgage must also be underwater, meaning that the property is worth less than the amount owed on the first mortgage. (If you owe $200,000 on your first mortgage, then the current value of your home typically must be less than that amount in order to get the bank to approve a settlement.)
- Each bank may have different requirements regarding what documents they will need to review in order to pursue a settlement (e.g., bank statements, pay stubs, a hardship letter, and a monthly expenses breakdown).
- Most junior liens will not settle out the account when the loan is a performing asset. This means that the homeowner typically needs to be sixty-plus days delinquent on payments prior to the bank allowing a settlement to be approved.
- If the homeowner has money in the bank, then the bank that owns your junior lien will want that money and may increase

the final settlement price. (If you have $5,000 in your bank account, the bank cannot expect you to give them $10,000 for a settlement, but if you have $20,000 in your account, the bank will want the majority of what you have to settle.)

- Anytime a homeowner has taken an income reduction or has relocated for employment reasons that can work to the homeowner's advantage. Losing household income as compared to past years can only help you to get your bank to work with you.

If you are unable to settle out the junior lien and are underwater $90,000, as in the above situation, that is not something that is recoverable in the short term. Any affluent, credit-conscious homeowner with a steady income would need to step back and reevaluate the situation. Typically when this happens, the next step would be pursuing the best exit strategy, which would lead to a short sale. We will go into more detail regarding short sales in Chapter 5.

CHAPTER 4

Other Options

Now that we have briefly discussed the options homeowners have when trying to retain their property, let's discuss other options that are available. These are viable options when retaining the property is not the goal and getting rid of the debt is the main objective. Many times the homeowner is being relocated for work, wants to move out of state, has grown out of the property, has seen the value drop significantly, no longer wants to be in the current neighborhood, or is unable to handle the costs associated with homeownership.

We're going to break down these options and go over why each one may be a better option than a home retention program, depending on each individual predicament. Whether you have found yourself owing significantly more on your home than it is worth or you just want to get out of a property you are no longer interested in owning and cannot sell it as a traditional sale due to its current value, identifying the best exit strategy is the best direction for you and your family in the long term.

Short Sale

Generally the most beneficial option when it comes down to getting rid of a property that is overleveraged is a short sale. A short sale is when a homeowner and mortgage company work together and, through negotiations, the bank agrees to accept less than the amount owed on the current loan, by allowing the property to be sold to a third-party buyer. The short sale process is different for each bank and will require the homeowner to submit numerous financial documents so the bank is able to complete its internal due diligence in evaluating the situation.

Short sales are the most widely used option when a homeowner is trying to get rid of a property that is overleveraged because it is typically the most beneficial option for all parties. Although the banks are taking a loss on the mortgage for each short sale, they are also minimizing their losses due to the additional costs and risks associated with the other options. In a short sale, you are allowing an interested buyer and motivated seller to work together to transfer ownership of a property, and all parties cooperate with each other to reach the desired outcome.

Another benefit of a short sale is that the risk of a homeowner being disgruntled and purposefully damaging the property is dramatically reduced. A deteriorating property is another risk these banks take when they foreclose on a property rather than agree to a short sale. The deterioration/destruction of the property condition is less likely when pursuing a short sale as opposed to the homeowner just walking away from the problem and forcing the bank to move forward with the costly foreclosure process. Keeping the property in better condition also helps the neighborhood retain its value.

The benefits to the banks of a short sale option are obvious. As a short sale, it enables them to reduce the other possible costs associated with foreclosure and owning real estate, which is not what these banks want.

The homeowner also benefits in numerous ways. In a short sale, the seller wants to get out of a negative-equity situation and get into a better financial position long term. At the same time, most sellers also want to minimize the credit hit associated with losing the property. This is important, and homeowners can minimize the derogatory hit to their credit by working toward a short sale, as opposed to walking away from the property and allowing the bank to drag it out as long as it wants.

When working toward a short sale, the homeowners is required to submit specific documents that their bank requires and will have to endure the frustrating short sale review process. The time frame for getting through a short sale fluctuates significantly. Over the last few years, my staff and I have successfully negotiated nearly four thousand short sale approvals and currently have an average time frame of -54 days to get all liens approved. This time frame starts when we receive the executed purchase agreement and runs until we have secured all lien approvals on the property to move forward with closing. Obviously short sales are anything but short, but, considering the benefits to the homeowner, I think the frustrating processing time is a small price to pay if indeed it gives the homeowner the ability to get out of a large mortgage obligation.

Short sales also enable homeowners to have some element of control, since they always have the ability to cancel the transaction and because short sales enable homeowners to have clarity on the final terms. These are two key components that make the short sale option extremely attractive for homeowners. Maybe homeowners don't control the banks' internal review processes for a short sale approval, but they do have the ability to cancel the transaction and move in another direction if the bank doesn't work with them or is offering unreasonable terms.

As a homeowner who was personally in the situation of being under-water significantly on my home, I wanted to see what the bank would offer me so that I could then decide whether their offer was accept-able or not. I am also located in Nevada, which is a bank-friendly state that gives the bank the ability to pursue a homeowner personally after a short sale or foreclosure. Based on that I wanted to be clear on what the final terms of the transaction were as opposed to being completely in the dark as I would have been if indeed I had just ignored the problem and allowed the bank to foreclose on the property.

This was one of the main reasons I chose to short sell my personal property. The approval I received made it very clear that once I closed the transaction, the bank would then waive its legal right to pursue me in the future for the outstanding balance owed. This is what I mean when I say clarity. I was very clear on what the final approved terms were and was very comfortable moving forward. I had to give the bank a capital contribution at closing, but the amount of money I was required to pay them after negotiations was minimal compared to the benefit I received by getting out of a property that was underwater over $200,000.

At the end of the day, pursuing a short sale is in most cases the best direction for homeowners whose goal is to be relieved of the financial obligation associated with an underwater mortgage. Short sales give them both control of moving forward or not as well as clarity on what the terms of the transaction are. In a short sale, the bank may want a contribution from the homeowner at closing, but as long as the homeowner is getting the best bang for the buck, I don't see that as unreasonable. In some cases the bank wants the homeowner to contribute toward the loss they are taking. In other cases the bank is withholding their right to pursue the outstanding balance owed after closing. Either way, being able to see the terms outlined in front of them puts homeowners in a better position to make a decision on how to move forward.

Below I have outlined a few outcomes we have secured for our clients who were in extreme situations and what the final terms were for these clients after negotiations. These extreme examples show that even when a homeowner does generate a high amount of income, they can still pursue a short sale. (Examples of more average situations are included in the back of the book.)

Example #1

Homeowners' combined monthly income:	**$90,000**
Amount owed on the current mortgage:	**$792,000**
Amount of the offer to purchase the property:	**$528,000**

Terms of the transaction at closing:

As terms of the negotiated short sale approval, the bank required that the seller pay $62,673 at the closing table but agreed to accept a loss of ~$200,000. As terms of the approval, the bank also waived its legal right to pursue the seller personally for the outstanding balance owed so that the seller could move on without any risk of the bank pursing them in the future.

Example #2

Homeowners' combined monthly income:	**$24,000**
Amount owed on the current mortgage:	**$624,000**
Amount of the offer to purchase the property:	**$295,000**

Terms of the transaction at closing:

As part of the negotiations on this file, the sellers were not required to bring in any money to closing. They had the financial means to make the payments (see the monthly income line), but the property was so underwater that they decided that retaining it would only be throwing away more money. As terms of the approval, the bank waived its legal right to pursue the outstanding balance (~$330,000) from the seller.

Example #3

Homeowners' combined monthly income:	**$65,000**
Amount owed on the current mortgage:	**$1,330,000**
Amount of the offer to purchase the property:	**$650,000**

Terms of the transaction at closing:

Through negotiations we were able to negotiate the short sale approval and the homeowners were not required to bring in any capital contribution at closing. The sellers were relieved of nearly $700,000 in negative equity, while also getting the bank to waive its legal right to pursue them personally for the outstanding amount owed.

Example #4

Homeowners' combined monthly income:	**$120,000**
Amount owed on the current mortgage:	**$440,000**
Amount of the offer to purchase the property:	**$150,000**

Terms of the transaction at closing:

Within this negotiated short sale approval, the bank approved the transaction without any contribution being required from the sellers and agreed to absorb the loss of nearly $310,000. As terms of the approval, the bank also waived its legal right to pursue the sellers for the outstanding balance owed.

Since a short sale is the most commonly pursued option, we'll go into more detail on the short sale process with the different banks in Chapter 5.

Possible Negatives of a Short Sale:

- The seller will be required to submit certain financial documents to the bank.
- Time frame to get through a short sale may fluctuate significantly on each transaction. (Short sales have taken as long as fifteen months to complete, but typical turnaround times range from two to five months depending on the bank servicing the loan.
- Bank may want a capital contribution or promissory note from the seller.
- No guarantees that a bank will approve a short sale.
- Possible tax liability associated with the short sale, depending on the specifics of each situation. (When a bank takes a loss on a mortgage, they will typically issue a 1099. That 1099 may also come with a phantom income tax, depending on the occupancy of the property and whether the money owed was used to purchase/upgrade the property or was a cash-out refinance for personal use.)

Every short sale situation is different; the final terms of the transaction will be dictated by each individual seller's circumstances and by who is negotiating with the bank. This is why aligning yourself with a team of experienced professionals is so critical if you are in a situation where you decide to short sell your home. These professionals will be able to ensure that homeowners have reasonable expectations from the onset based on their unique circumstances. When homeowners align themselves with inexperienced people to handle the transaction, the only people at risk are the homeowners. Working with people who don't have a specific skill set in short sales reduces the likelihood of getting the best possible terms on the transaction and increases the probability that the short sale will not be approved.

Deed In Lieu of Foreclosure (DIL)

The deed in lieu of foreclosure option is not very prevalent but is an option that some homeowners have. A DIL is essentially when the bank agrees to allow a homeowner to turn over the keys and takes the property back without needing to go through the foreclosure process. In order to qualify for this option, all lienholders on the property would need to approve the DIL—and that is very unlikely, even when the same bank is servicing both liens. With multiple liens on the property, the deed in lieu of foreclosure is typically not an option.

This option does benefit the bank, as it enables the bank to avoid the possible risks and costs associated with going through the foreclosure process, but this option is also a negative to the bank because if the bank approves a DIL, the bank takes over responsibility for the property once the DIL is final. This is not an attractive option for banks, as they do not want to own real estate or take on the additional responsibilities associated with maintaining the property. If they approve a DIL, then they are responsible for anything that may happen to the property. If someone were to get hurt on the property, the bank would be responsible. That is a real risk and a driving factor for banks' reluctance to approve DILs over the last few years. Additionally, if the bank does take over ownership, then it is also responsible for the upkeep of the property. That upkeep tends to add up quickly as property taxes, homeowners insurance, landscaping, and Homeowners Association (HOA) fees continue adding up while the bank is trying to secure a buyer for the property.

The deed in lieu of foreclosure option benefits the homeowners by enabling them to avoid the long, drawn-out process of a foreclosure and, in some cases, enabling them to negotiate a deficiency waiver as terms of the DIL. A deficiency waiver is when the bank waives its rights to pursue the homeowner personally in the future for the loss they take. This enables the homeowners to move on without fear of the bank pursuing them after the fact for the outstanding balance owed.

To qualify for a DIL, most banks have specific guidelines that must be met. Typically a bank will not accept a DIL until homeowners show that they have actively attempted to sell the property on the open market through a real estate agent for a minimum of ninety days. The home must also be on the market at a price considered to be a true fair market value based on recent sales of similar homes in the area. The banks want to make sure homeowners have tried to do their part before they would ever allow a DIL to be accepted. The banks would also gather certain financial documents from the homeowners, along with a hardship letter outlining the circumstances the homeowners may be in that make retaining the property impossible.

We have completed a handful of DILs for our clients over the last few years, and in my opinion this option is not worth pursuing until you have already pursued a short sale for a minimum of four months. The DILs we have completed were all on properties that were damaged to the point that getting a buyer interested in submitting a fair market offer was nearly impossible. The repairs needed were going to be so costly that, after months of getting no interest or getting low offers due to the condition of these properties, the bank finally just agreed to accept the DIL.

I would assume the banks decided that they wanted first to confirm these damages were real and planned to then have their own people repair them. Once they made the repairs, the bank resells these properties on the open market. In my opinion, it would have made more sense to accept a lower offer on each of these properties and let someone else complete the repairs, but banks typically fear that the damages are not real and that they are being misled as to the actual condition of the property.

This may be a valid fear the banks have, as buyers and real estate agents are trying to get the banks to approve short sales for less than the current value by fraudulently submitting inaccurate damage reports. I have never encountered this issue myself but have heard of this happening and have also spoken to bank representatives who have confirmed it is happening a lot. As a result, the banks are forced to tighten up internal guidelines, which makes it more difficult when it comes to these issues.

Obviously many factors may be involved in getting a DIL approved, and in most cases it is just not happening. The DIL is an option, but really an option that is rarely approved by the banks. Below are a few downsides of a DIL:

Possible Negatives of a Deed In Lieu of Foreclosure:

- Requires effort on the sellers' side.
- Unlikely to happen, so it is best to first pursue a short sale.
- Has the same negatives as a foreclosure for the homeowner (discussed in the following section).

Foreclosure

A homeowner always has the option of doing nothing at all and allowing the bank to foreclose on the property. All the homeowner has to do is stop making the payments and ignore the bank's calls and letters acknowledging the delinquency. This is not the preferred method for the banks and in most cases is not the best option for the homeowner either. If indeed the homeowners decide to go this direction, they need to take into consideration many other factors before just defaulting and allowing a foreclosure to take place.

Can banks pursue the homeowner personally after they foreclose on the property? The answer to this question depends on whether the property is located in a recourse or non-recourse state. Some states are recourse states, meaning that the bank does have the option to come after homeowners personally for the amount of the loss they took as a result of the foreclosure. Some states are non-recourse, meaning the bank does not have the legal right to pursue a homeowner personally after a foreclosure has taken place. In non-recourse states all the bank can do is take back the collateral used when issuing the loan. Sometimes these laws are specific to only the senior lien (i.e., the first mortgage), and then the junior lien(s) (i.e., any other liens behind the senior lien) may be handled differently. The law may also be specific as to whether the loan was an equity line of credit, a purchase money loan used at the time of purchase, or a refinance loan. A cash-out refinance, as opposed to a rate-and-term refinance, may also change the risk homeowners may face if indeed they decide to walk away from the problem rather than face it head on through a short sale.

As a homeowner, understanding the law in your state is important to making a decision on which is the best option based on your predicament. By educating yourself up front, you are putting yourself in a better position to make a long-term decision you won't regret.

Realistically, a foreclosure should be an alternative after the homeowners have already tried to pursue a short sale. If the homeowners can get a short sale approved and negotiate the best terms possible, then they should try to pursue that option first. If for some reason the bank denies the homeowners' short sale request or wants unreasonable terms as part of the short sale, the homeowners can then default and go in the direction of a foreclosure.

Based on the fact that a short sale is an option that would minimize the derogatory credit hit to the homeowners and would also give them the ability to have complete clarity as to the terms of the transaction, a foreclosure is rarely the preferred option—nor should it be. A short sale is a better option in most cases for obvious reasons discussed in the preceding section, but if the bank reviewing the short sale is being unreasonable, homeowners can change gears and go in the direction of a foreclosure. Sometimes a foreclosure may be unavoidable, depending on the homeowners' situation. However it is always good to consider pursuing the short sale first so that the homeowners know they tried everything to work with the bank in attempt to minimize the hit they will inevitably take.

When homeowners allow a property to go into foreclosure, two concerns are completely out of their control:

1. When will the bank finally foreclose on the property?

What if the bank does not foreclose for ten-plus months? The homeowners' credit is getting thrashed all the way until the foreclosure is final. This puts the homeowners in a position of having no control and taking a much larger credit hit than they would have in a short sale scenario.

2. Will the bank come after the homeowner in the future?

Just because the bank forecloses on a home doesn't mean they will end up coming after the homeowner in the future for the amount of its loss plus all the fees associated with the foreclosure process, but it is possible and it does happen. In a short sale, the homeowners have the ability to negotiate the terms of the transaction, which means that there is no uncertainty and they can move on with their life knowing exactly what exposure they may or may not have. In a foreclosure, homeowners are essentially in a dark room and they are at the banks mercy as to when it will foreclose and whether they will come after them in the future, which is not a comfortable situation. This is why the foreclosure option should rarely be the first option that a homeowner considers. Instead, it should be a backup plan in case a short sale or other foreclosure alternative does not get approved with acceptable terms.

Besides the negative aspects listed above, foreclosures are not the direction the banks typically want to go in either. A foreclosure nets the bank significantly less than any of the alternatives. The reason this is the worst-case outcome for the bank / investor who owns these assets is that they have to absorb transaction fees, delinquent taxes, delinquent hazard insurance, and everything else associated with the homeowners just walking away from the property. On top of that, they still have to absorb attorney fees for facilitating a foreclosure—and those fees can add up in a hurry.

Other unpredictable costs associated with a foreclosure can also add up to a significant amount. Many of these homeowners who are walking away from their homes are also damaging these properties on their way out. A lot of them are disgruntled and feeling duped by the banks. These homeowners are sometimes not only victims of the current economy but also feel as if they were taken advantage of by the banks when they were issued a mortgage that they could not truly afford. They see the fraudulent appraisal activities and predatory loan programs (that enabled them to get into the situation) as being manufactured by the banks and in some cases are doing irrational things out of frustration.

Whether it's right or wrong, it is a reality of what is taking place in some markets throughout the country and something that costs the banks a considerable amount of money. I have heard of homeowners damaging properties to the point of putting liquid cement in the pipes, breaking walls, breaking doors, damaging landscaping, removing countertops/cabinets, flooding the home, and numerous other things that would all need to be repaired if indeed the bank wants to turn around and get the home sold on the open market. The repairs come at a cost that will end up being absorbed by the bank in a foreclosure, but could have possibly been avoided in a short sale. The bank can hold the homeowner liable for any damages and may pursue them for the costs of repairing these damages plus, attorney fees.

Another issue that comes up when banks look at foreclosures would be the time frame to complete the transaction. Everything is based on the home's current value, and the longer it takes to get through the process of a foreclosure, the higher the probability that the property will continue to deteriorate in condition and value. If the foreclosure process takes ten months, then the bank can in most cases also expect that the homeowners have not maintained the home. The longer the foreclosure process takes to complete, the more deterioration of the property condition is expected. Getting the home back into resale shape and then maintaining it costs the bank more money than simply working with the homeowners on approving a short sale.

Negatives of a Foreclosure:

- Even more drawn-out process to finalize
- Typically a more significant credit hit for homeowners
- Homeowners may have increased future exposure/risk of the bank pursuing them personally for the loss plus the costs associated with the foreclosure process
- Lack of both control and clarity for homeowners as to what is going on behind the scenes.
- Could be a long term problem for people who are employed or plan on being employed in certain industries that require employee credit checks

Bankruptcy

In most cases, the last exit option homeowners should consider when they find themselves in an underwater property would be filing for bankruptcy. The reason bankruptcy is such a popular option is because bankruptcy attorneys are in many cases portraying it as the only option. Homeowners have been routinely told that it is the best option for them to address an underwater mortgage. The reality is that bankruptcy is a very good option when the homeowner also has other debts that also need to be addressed in addition to an underwater mortgage. With a bankruptcy, they can essentially take care of everything all at once.

When the main debt that a homeowner needs to address is an underwater mortgage, then one of the other options would make more sense for them and a bankruptcy should be considered as a last resort. The other options that have been discussed in this chapter may offer relief to the homeowners so they can achieve their goal and at the same time avoid filing for bankruptcy. If, for some reason, attempts to move forward with another option fail, then the homeowners could use the bankruptcy as a last resort to ensure they get rid of the debt associated with the underwater mortgage and any personal exposure that may accompany it.

Is a bankruptcy the best direction? This is a question I get asked quite often, and the answer really is completely dictated by the individual situation. If you have other obligations that are also going to be an issue regardless of your real estate holdings, then a bankruptcy may be the right direction from the onset. If you don't have other obligations then you should not even consider it as an option until you have pursued one of the other alternatives. If the bank will not work with you on a short sale, or they have approved the short sale but then decided to pursue you personally for the outstanding amount owed (if this is indeed possible in your state), then a bankruptcy can be a viable option.

Another scenario where it may make sense to file for bankruptcy would be just prior to a foreclosure sale date. This is sometimes a beneficial tactic for homeowners who are in an extreme hardship, to delay the foreclosure process. Filing bankruptcy puts a stay or freeze on all assets including the home. Due to the stay on the assets the foreclosure cannot continue and must be placed on hold until the bankruptcy is completed or the bank receives court ordered approval to continue the process. This allows the homeowner to continue living in the property for a longer period of time without making payments while the bankruptcy gets finalized. Most people want to have closure to the problem so that they can move on, but others have found themselves unemployed or in a situation where having a roof over their heads is the main goal until they can get back on their feet.

Once the homeowner has filed for bankruptcy, all collection activities are put on hold until the bankruptcy gets discharged. Once the bankruptcy is completed or the bank files a motion with the court for a lift of stay on the mortgage asset, then the foreclosure can again move forward. (Keep in mind, it will move forward from the point it was halted as a result of the bankruptcy filing – the clock does not start over – if a sale date was on the horizon the property could potentially go right to sale depending on the state laws where the property is located) Usually this process takes months to complete and this is why it can be a beneficial option for homeowners who are facing an extreme hardship. After a homeowner has included a property in a bankruptcy and the bankruptcy is completed / dismissed, the bank will again be able to move forward with the foreclosure process in order to take back the property and then re-sell it in order to recapture some of the money that was owed.

Negatives of a Bankruptcy:

- Typically not needed if the property is the homeowners' main or only debt
- Qualifying for a bankruptcy is not as easy as it may have been in the past
- Homeowners who file Chapter 13 bankruptcy are obligated to make monthly payments to the court for a number of years
- May be more of a negative in the future when homeowners want to purchase another property or borrow credit again
- Draws out the process of having closure and starting over for the homeowner
- Could be a long term problem for people who are employed or plan on being employed in certain industries that require employee credit checks

In order to summarize these options I want to emphasize that the short sale option is the most often used because it is the most beneficial option in the vast majority of cases for all parties involved. Due to the fact that every situation is completely different, the right option for you may not be the right option for someone else and that is why understanding each option is important. Understanding the options should enable each individual to determine how to address their problem based on their specific circumstances and goals.

Over the last 5 years we have successfully closed on nearly 90 percent of the short sales we have been involved with. During that same time the amount of transactions we have lost to foreclosure is estimated to be 7 percent and the number of clients we have seen forced into a bankruptcy would be less than 3 percent. Although these numbers don't capture the entire industry, they do represent a large number of files and they clearly outline the fact that banks want to pursue short sales and are working with homeowners to achieve a mutually beneficial outcome while avoiding bankruptcy and foreclosure as often as possible.

After a foreclosure the bank may be willing to give a homeowner still occupying the property "Cash for Keys" which is money to help them relocate. This program is similar to the seller incentive offered through some short sale programs and something the bank often offers to homeowners who have kept the property in good condition throughout the foreclosure process as opposed to damaging it. Cash for keys is typically $500-$3,000.

After a foreclosure takes place or a short sale is completed and the bank does not waive their legal right to pursue the homeowner personally for the remainder of the debt, and the bank does pursue the homeowner for that loss, at that point the homeowner could file for bankruptcy. This is something that we have been able to avoid in the majority of cases by being successful in getting our clients approved for one of the other options.

Even in the situations where a short sale was successful but the bank did not waive their legal right to pursue the homeowner in the future for the outstanding balance owed, many of these homeowners never ended up actually getting pursued. Since they were not pursued for the outstanding balance they had no reason to file for bankruptcy. In the majority of cases up to this point, the bank has chosen to get the tax benefit associated with writing off the loss and issuing the homeowner a 1099 at the end of the year. This means that the bank decided that getting the tax benefit from issuing the 1099 and writing off that loss was in their best interest as opposed to pursuing the homeowner personally for the loss. I don't think this will be the case moving forward as the banks are getting more organized internally and in my opinion, are going to start pursuing homeowners more often. We have at this point experienced a very small percentage of cases where this has taken place.

CHAPTER 5

The Evolution of Short Sales

A s outlined in the previous chapters, homeowners have options that will enable them to in some cases reduce their monthly expenses associated with their mortgages. In more severe situations, they also have options geared more toward getting rid of a bad mortgage along with the overall debt associated with it. Home retention programs are available, but when getting out of the financial obligation of a mortgage is the goal, the preferred method of accomplishing that goal for both banks and homeowners is a short sale.

Short sales have evolved extensively in the last five years but they are still tedious transactions with many moving pieces. In order to get through a short sale successfully, all the moving pieces associated with each particular transaction need to come together. In this chapter, I will explain first where we have been and then second, I will explain the direction we are moving. As a result, I hope to help educate homeowners and realtors so they are better prepared for the short sale process and can combat the hurdles that routinely get in the way.

Based on the reality that short sales in high numbers were basically forced upon us, other things also had to change. Due to the huge demand of these relatively new transactions, homeowners, banks, and real estate professionals were all forced to evolve their business. In addition, everyone had to try to understand the complexities of these transactions so they could try to work together to make sure that all parties could in the end, secure their individual goals. Sellers obviously wanted to get out of a bad mortgage buyers wanted to purchase a particular property and banks wanted to avoid the long and rather costly process of inevitable foreclosures in the future.

Even though it may seem as if the banks were the bottleneck, they were simply not in a position to handle the volume of transactions that they were receiving and needed time to wrap their arms around the problem. They needed to train staff and set up what was in most cases, a brand new department. They also had to discuss how the different investors who actually owned these mortgages wanted them to handle the loans owned by each individual investor.

Remember that the loans are not owned by the bank or servicing company that the homeowners' monthly payments go to. The payments are typically sent to a servicing company whose responsibility is to service the loan so that the real investor (i.e., the owner of the mortgage) does not have to deal with each individual homeowner or problem that may surface. The investor gives the bank (i.e., the servicing company) certain delegated authority that will dictate exactly what the bank can or cannot do on the loans that they own. This is something that caused many issues in the beginning of the collapse and still continues to cause problems today. Let's explore this relationship in more detail.

Banks (Servicers) vs. Investors (Owners)

The homeowners make monthly payments to a company or bank that they commonly assume is also the owner of the mortgage and makes the decisions regarding the loan. In most cases, this is not accurate. The bank is only servicing the loan for the end investor who is the real owner of the mortgage. Bank of America, for instance, is the largest servicer of mortgages in the country. Wells Fargo, Chase, Citibank, and GMAC are also very large servicing companies. On average, it is estimated that less than 10 percent of all mortgages are both owned and serviced by the same bank. The owners of these mortgages are in most cases Fannie Mae or Freddie Mac, but they can also be a variety of other investment groups that purchased the mortgages. These are investors who want to minimize the losses they will inevitably take on these portfolios of mortgages.

Even though the banks routinely get a bad rap in the media for being so difficult and unwilling to move short sales forward, it is a combination of things that may not really be in the banks' control or their fault. Every investment group has its own ideas as to how to handle the problem, and that was and continues to cause serious confusion for everyone. It also plays a huge factor in what causes frustrations for sellers, real estate agents and buyers. These investors have been working with the banks and the government in attempt to create a more standardized way of doing things, but getting everyone to agree on how to handle this problem has always been a moving target when it comes to getting short sales approved and closed.

The Beginning of Short Sales

As the real estate market collapsed and mortgages were defaulting at such high rates, short sales were to a certain extent, forced to become part of many markets. Most homeowners were not aware of this option and instead decided to just walk away from their properties allowing foreclosures to take place, while others heard about short sales and saw them as a better option. These homeowners wanted to pursue the short sale option, but it was still somewhat uncharted territory. Homeowners had no idea as to what they would encounter going through the process, what the qualifying criteria was, how long it would take or who to go to for accurate information based on the details of their individual predicaments. They didn't have any experts to help them and educate them because no one had any experience. Everyone was basically trying to familiarize themselves with the whole concept. Most reverted to reading about short sales on the internet, which was and still is full of inaccurate or misleading information that has nothing to do with the specifics of what each individual homeowner may be dealing with. I am not saying that everything online is inaccurate. I am simply making the point that everyone has a different set of circumstances; therefore, what you are reading may be entirely inaccurate based on your specific situation.

Many people thought they could not short sell a property unless they were in serious financial hardship. They also didn't think they could short sell an investment property or vacation home. The reality is that, depending on the situation, you can short sell properties of any occupancy and in some cases a hardship may not truly be required. Yes, most banks want to see a hardship letter outlining the reason you cannot retain your home, but what is a hardship situation? Do you need to be unemployed? What if you were relocated for work? What if your neighborhood has deteriorated and you wanted to move? Is it really a hardship if you got overleveraged with real estate during the boom and took advantage of the loan programs available at the time? These are all questions people had but no one seemed to really have any answers in the beginning.

As the demand for short sales increased, the banks were also caught off guard and were essentially forced to staff up and train people to handle the overwhelming number of short sale requests they were receiving. They had to quickly establish an internal short sale review process and a list of required documents that had to be submitted by the seller within the short sale packet. They needed to make sure that they were getting certain information in order to show the end investors that they had done their proper due diligence prior to approving losses on the loans they were servicing.

It seemed that the same basic financials were needed for each short sale, but every bank would tweak them in their own way. In some cases what forms were needed was dictated by the investor who actually owned the loan. This caused a lot of problems for the simple fact that if an authorized third party was handling a short sale with a specific bank and then had another one with that same bank two weeks later, they may be asked for completely different things. In the mind of the person working for the consumer trying to get the short sale closed, it was very confusing why the same bank would want different documents or in some cases wanted the file submitted in an entirely different way.

Early in the short sale craze it seemed that the individual bank requirements were constantly changing and that the process of submitting the short sale requests was also changing every few months. This lack of a clear-cut process caused frustrations for everyone. Some banks would have you fax documents over to them while others would have you e-mail them over in order to get short sale submissions logged into their internal systems. Some banks were so bad at receiving the short sale packages that the same package was mailed to them with return-receipt confirmation in attempt to create a level of accountability. It seemed like every time you submitted documents to the bank, they would confirm receipt, but then a few days later they would say that the items were never added to the file and were still missing. This breakdown in communication internally at the banks was the main problem causing delays in the short sale review process and was also a huge contributor to the short sale process taking an average of fourteen months back in 2007-2009 as the short sale wave was beginning.

Just think for a minute how this process that took so long was frustrating the very people trying to facilitate a short sale, as opposed to just walking away from the problem and forcing the banks to foreclose on properties. These delays would also snowball into other issues, like buyers getting impatient and backing out of the transaction or homeowners getting disgruntled with the process and flat out walking away from the transaction after months of being forced to go in circles over and over again due to the lack of structure between the banks and investors who owned these loans. On top of taking an average of fourteen months to get through the process, it has been estimated that less than 50 percent of these short sale transactions were actually approved and closed.

The problem was so bad that the government had to step in and try to implement standards for everyone to meet. In September of 2009, after months of telling everyone that they were going to come out with a short sale program that would help expedite these transactions and finally establish a set of rules, the government came out with the Home Affordable Foreclosure Alternative program, otherwise known as HAFA. Leading up to the release of the program, homeowners, real estate agents, and third parties had high hopes of this program making a huge difference in the process. When the government finally came out with the qualifying criteria for the program, it became clear that it was not going to be the solution everyone had hoped for. The combination of strict guidelines and even more documents being required by HAFA just caused more confusion and inevitable delays. No one at the banks were ever held accountable for the endless number of mistakes being made and, because the banks were not properly staffing up or training employees, the misplacing of documents and blatant internal miscommunication continued. The program had good intentions, but was destined to fail from the beginning. HAFA even gave the banks the right to choose whether or not to participate, and most banks simply felt it was not worth participating due to the additional paperwork involved.

Initial HAFA Guidelines:

- The property had to be the homeowners' primary residence at the time of the short sale
- The debt-to-income ratios had to meet certain requirements
- It had certain asset restrictions, e.g., the homeowner could not have any significant funds in the bank
- Homeowners had to show a financial hardship, but because the details of each situation can be so unique it was difficult for them to see certain hardship as legitimate
- The banks who serviced the loan were not required to participate
- Junior lienholders would need to accept the amount they were allowed to receive as full settlement of the loan. They were only allowed to receive $3,000 in the initial program, regardless of the amount of money they were owed.

The guidelines did not require the banks to participate but it gave the banks the option to choose whether to participate in the HAFA program or not. Each bank could individually decide whether it wanted to participate and on what loans, based on the credits that it may receive. The problem with this was that even if the bank holding the first mortgage on the property did participate, the junior lienholder had to also participate in order for the program to work. However, most junior lien holders were not participating due to the small amount of money they would receive through the program. This was a very problematic piece of the puzzle because the process of being reviewed for the HAFA program was very time consuming. If the homeowner did actually get approved by the first lien holder, then the short sale negotiator working on behalf of the homeowner would go to the junior lien holder, who typically would say that they did not participate in HAFA and would not accept the amount of money the program allowed them to receive through the transaction.

So, after months of being reviewed for the program and getting the approval from the first lien holder, a homeowner was then forced to start the whole process from the beginning and pursue a normal short sale outside of the HAFA program. At that point the homeowner had already lost months and the buyer didn't want to stick around due to how long it was taking, or the property may be getting close to actually being foreclosed on. As discussed earlier, these delays may seem to be just a little thing, but the other issues that arose as a result caused the majority of short sales to fail.

Due to the strict guidelines and lack of structure for the HAFA program when it was initially released, it has been estimated that less than 20 percent of homeowners who applied for HAFA actually got approved and closed through the program. With such a low conversion rate, it was obvious that it was not going to be the fix everyone had hoped for. Many homeowners avoided the program from the onset in order to avoid the delays it caused. If it took many months to be reviewed for HAFA and the likelihood of getting approved was so low, why not just skip the program altogether and start working on a conventional short sale, which would take less time for the review and therefore reduce the other risks associated with long delays? The longer the process takes, the higher the risk of losing the buyer, getting foreclosed upon and possible further deterioration of the property.

Most homeowners wanted to do the right thing, but at the same time, they wanted to have a light at the end of the tunnel and did not want to continuously beat their head against a wall. The initial HAFA program was not necessarily helping them meet those goals, so instead they preferred to go in a different direction. Rather than go through the long HAFA review process, they would often rather negotiate the term of a conventional short sale to get to the finish line in a much more efficient and certain manner.

Benefits of the HAFA Program:

- If the homeowners were approved, they would be given a seller relocation incentive of up to $3,000 at closing. This was a way to help offset the relocation expenses for a homeowner in a hardship situation. (Other non-HAFA short sale programs may also include an element of a seller incentive.)

- If the homeowner was approved for the program, then the bank had to waive their legal rights to pursue the homeowner personally for the outstanding balance owed on the loan. (The terms of non-HAFA short sales are based on negotiations, where getting the bank to also waive their right to pursue the homeowner personally can also be attained.)
- Banks receive credits from the government for participating in the program.

Initial Problems with HAFA:

- Expectations in regards to what was being portrayed in the media prior to the release of the program gave everyone high hopes. Once the program was released, it became very clear that the program was not getting the expected results.
- Vague guidelines that seemed to be up to interpretation.
- Qualifying criteria was not clear to the banks or the consumers.
- Required many additional forms that in turn made the process more tedious and inefficient.
- Review process was taking much longer than anticipated and no one was held accountable for the many errors being made within the banks.
- Small percentage of applicants actually got approved for the program.
- Banks were reluctant to participate due to the strict requirements and little benefit they received for participating.
- Junior lienholders were not incentivized enough to cooperate with the program, even if the same bank did participate when they were in senior lien position.
- When denied for HAFA, the process of transitioning in the direction of a non-HAFA short sale was not efficient and caused further delays and frustrations for everyone.
- Program did not allow any money to go toward other liens that needed to be paid prior to closing. (property taxes, sewer demands homeowner association transfer costs, etc.)

Educating Homeowners and Real Estate Professionals

Since short sales have become prevalent in only the last five years, many homeowners and real estate professionals typically have false impressions of how they work. Short sales did happen in the past and have been around for much longer than five years, but they have never happened at this volume. This explains why there has been a learning curve for both consumers and the banks as they adapt to the evolving market. Homeowners fear the unknown, based merely on individual situations they have heard about, and real estate agents fear not performing for their clients. Many real estate agents also fear the potential liability associated with handling such a complex transaction due to the risk of it going sideways. For these reasons, I think many people have avoided short sales altogether. Instead they should be tackling the problem as opposed to avoiding it.

Homeowners need to understand that every situation is completely different and nothing they have heard or read may pertain to them at all. If homeowners are under the assumption that everything they have heard about short sales is a standard across the board and will pertain to them, their assumptions are inaccurate. The details of each situation are completely different and therefore have nothing to do with each other.

If you are a real estate agent, how can you operate a business from a standpoint of avoiding what may be a large percentage of transactions in your market? Agents cannot look at it as if you may be unable to perform or may get sued if the transaction falls apart at some point. Instead, agents should embrace the market they are in and try to capitalize on the opportunity to help the community. Many agents have chosen to avoid these transactions. In reality they should consider short sales as an excellent way to actually grow their business, while at the same time helping people who need to be educated and need their guidance. Agents don't have to pass on listings just because they are not familiar with how these transactions work. Instead they should evolve with the times and point these homeowners in the right direction, so they can assist distressed homeowners and address the problem. Maybe a certain number of transactions are destined to fail for a variety of reasons, but I see that as part of the challenge we all face and a challenge I am willing to take on to help homeowners who have found themselves in this unfortunate situation. I approach each transaction knowing that I cannot help everyone but also very confident that if anyone can navigate the transaction to a successful closing, it is my team.

Due to the severity of these recent changes, homeowners and real estate professionals need to become educated on the short sale process and the complexities of these transactions. By doing so, they will increase the likelihood of getting to the desired outcome for their clients. Short sales are very tedious and frustrating, but understanding the critical pieces of these transactions will only increase the probability of getting them closed and help reduce the stress associated with the whole process for everyone involved.

As homeowners become more educated and as real estate professionals / third parties gain the experience that comes with being in the trenches of dealing with short sales on a daily basis, we are all more likely to overcome the numerous obstacles that routinely get in the way. Hopefully the information in this chapter will enable both homeowners and the professionals working on their behalf to position each transaction for a successful outcome by helping them understand the critical pieces of a short sale and therefore avoiding many problems before they surface.

Below is a list of the critical components of a short sale that are in your control and need to be understood from the onset. *These work for both real estate agents and homeowners.*

Critical Pieces of Short Sales

Aligning Yourself with the Right Team of Professionals

As a homeowner you need to do your homework and identify the right team of professionals to work with. It is in your best interest to make sure they are experienced with short sales and in turn, their involvement will increase the probability of getting your short sale approved. It does not mean that you are guaranteed a successful outcome, but at the end of the day you need to have confidence that they do have the right skill set to navigate through the process on your behalf. You have to trust them to do what they have been hired to do and cannot second guess this decision after the fact. Once you make the decision to move forward with your selected professionals, you have to work together as a team and always be on the same page.

In the last few years I have always found this as the most important piece to a successful, stress-free transaction, and as we have gained more clients and more experience, the importance of working with the right people has only been emphasized more. This is due to the overwhelming number of homeowners that have come to us after already working with someone else who not only failed to achieve the short sale approval, but also failed to communicate to the client and explain what was going on. Inevitably the homeowner seeks other opinions as they slowly lose confidence that the person they were working with has the skill set to cross the finish line. In my experience, the transaction we have worked on after someone else had already been communicating and submitting documents to the bank, we routinely encounter issues that could have been avoided if indeed the other person had an idea of what they were doing. In most cases we are able to pick up the pieces but sometimes what has already been done cannot be undone. That is why it is critical for homeowners to select the right team of professionals to take on the transaction. In order to select the right professionals to work with, you have two key decisions to make:

1. Who do you want to be handling the day-to-day communication with the bank(s)?

At this point you really have four options of who will be handling the communication with the banks. These options are having a (1) real estate agent, (2) an attorney, (3) a licensed third party, or (4) a title company take on that responsibility. Do not be persuaded by certifications or legal titles that some of these options may have but instead focus on the experience that each brings to the table. For example, you may want to ask how many short sales they have handled in the last two years. Instead of reviewing the classes they have taken or certifications they may have, consider the their real-life experiences dealing with these banks. If someone has handled ten short sales this year and converted on all of them, does that mean that their 100 percent conversion rate is more enticing than someone who has secured a thousand short sale approvals but is only converting 90 percent of them? Absolutely not, it only means that they have encountered very few issues and don't have the experience that would be needed if your transaction encountered problems. Experience matters most in an industry that is constantly changing. This is the key to making the best decision as to who you hire to handle your short sale and deal with your bank.

These same points also pertain to real estate professionals who have been taking on short sales or who are just now entering that market. You have to ask yourself whether you are the best person to be dealing with the banks and if you have the time it requires to handle the behind-the-scenes, tedious process. Does your skillset enhance the probability of closing the transaction? Does your assistant bring to the table the experience you trust to get your client to the finish line? Does taking on the additional expense of hiring someone to handle these transactions make sense, or does it make more sense to outsource that part to a third party? How does handling these transactions internally increase the likelihood of closing for your clients? Does handling this piece of the transaction increase your income or does it actually reduce it as a result of not having time to pursue other business opportunities?

It is easy to see the benefit of outsourcing to an experienced third party. It enables you to focus on building your pipeline of business (both buyers and sellers) while utilizing someone else's expertise to ensure that the transactions close. You just have to select the best third party based on the same factors outlined above, so you are confident that the third party you work with is experienced and increasing the likelihood of getting the transaction closed. Experience is truly the key element in getting short sale transactions successfully processed and approved.

I remember the learning curve for my staff as we encountered issues that would routinely surface when dealing with short sales. Our learning curve was reduced somewhat thanks to the sheer volume of transactions we were handling. By handling hundreds of transactions at a time, we were able to quickly learn how to deal with the numerous different banks and how to properly structure a file from the onset so we could avoid some of the issues that were causing delays. This experience far exceeds what most real estate agents or attorneys could ever have since they are also trying to juggle other aspects of their businesses. Gaining that type of experience does not happen unless you are 100 percent focused on just dealing with the banks and securing short sale approvals, which is what we have been doing for nearly five years and the reason why we have secured so many short sale approvals.

2.   Who will list your property for sale and secure a buyer?

After you identify the key professional who will be handling the dealings with the bank(s), you need to decide who will list your property for sale, market the property and secure a legitimate buyer at a price that is in line with the fair market value. This means that you will need to find a real estate professional to handle what they have been trained to do. Although this may seem to be a simple thing, it most definitely is not. You cannot entrust just anyone to help you get through this tedious process, especially when you have a huge mortgage obligation at stake.

Once again, experience is the key to aligning yourself with the right team. Getting offers and identifying the one with the highest probability of a patient and committed buyer who is willing to wait the process out is extremely important. Maybe it is not the cash offer or the highest offer that you want to accept. Having a real estate professional who knows how to identify the best offer on a short sale is critical if you want to avoid frustration later on in the transaction. Another key component of the real estate professional you choose is that he or she needs to keep the buyer updated throughout the process so that the buyer is not left in the dark. You want the buyer to be updated so that he or she is always motivated to move forward. If communication between your real estate professional and the buyer is lacking, then you run the real risk of the buyer finding another home, which means that you will be forced to start over and find another buyer.

Other factors go into selecting your real estate professional, but always remember that these transactions are not typical and that small things might snowball into larger issues if the person you are working with fails to understand the complexities of these transactions. Do not put any value on short sale certifications or how long the person has been in the real estate industry, as neither truly matters. Identify someone who has real experience handling short sale transactions. In many cases, the real estate agents who have been around for many years may be stuck in the old ways of doing business and not evolved into handling short sales.

Consider it a red flag when real estate agents say they do everything themselves. More than likely that is a sign that they lack experience. How could they properly service other clients or cultivate new buyer or seller leads if they are doing everything themselves? Real estate agents cannot do everything themselves and handle the number of transactions it takes to really gain the experience a homeowner should require from them. This lack of a team approach and real-world experience that many agents have only reduces the probability of them helping the homeowner (you) get to the desired outcome. Over the last few years short sales have failed to close an estimated 50 percent of the time, as opposed to what we have experienced in closing closer to 90 percent of the transactions we have handled through a team approach. That reality makes working with a team clearly much more beneficial and well worth any additional costs.

As a homeowner who went through a short sale on my personal property, I understand the fear of the unknown and the stress associated with the whole process. I also understand the complexities of each transaction and the amount of work it takes to cross the finish line with the best possible terms. Would you as a homeowner rather have a "free" service, even though as a result the transaction may be delayed or the terms of the transaction may not be the best you could have gotten?

I specifically remember a transaction that came to me after already being worked through a law firm for nearly eight months. The attorney had not secured an approval or communicated with the other parties within the transaction, leaving them completely in the dark. The homeowner decided to cancel the file with the law firm (walking away from the $3,500 fee they had already paid) and had my firm take it over. We were familiar with that particular bank and used a contact we had gained working with them on previous transactions to get an expedited approval within thirty days. Obviously the benefit of having a true specialist involved was huge and kept this transaction together before the buyer cancelled which would have and forced everyone to start over from the beginning or could have possibly resulted in a foreclosure.

On another transaction that was being handled by a title company in what they called a "free" short sale negotiation/processing service, the homeowner was being asked to sign a $30,000 promissory note as terms of the negotiated short sale approval. The homeowner wanted to avoid being stuck with this long-term responsibility and decided to have my firm take the file over. We negotiated the same transaction but were able to get the bank to accept a one-time cash contribution in the amount of $3,100 at closing. This was obviously much more beneficial for the homeowner than the $30,000 promissory note that was negotiated through the "free" title company short sale negotiation/processing service. Our fee was minimal in comparison to the promissory note and the homeowner felt the fee was reasonable considering the end result.

Realistic Expectations from the Onset

Everyone has a different set of circumstances in regard to their mortgage situation, income, assets, employment, and other miscellaneous issues that will factor into what the outcome may be. Prior to moving forward with a short sale, make sure you are working with someone who has the most experience dealing with similar situations. If the person you are working with constantly talks about experience with your bank, that should be a red flag. It is not the bank necessarily that matters, but the owner of the mortgage behind the scenes and what type of loan (conventional, FHA, or VA) a homeowner may have. The specifics of each situation will enable someone with experience to set an expectation with a homeowner so that everyone can avoid surprises down the road. This all goes back to whom you choose to work with and their ability to set accurate expectations based on the following details:

- Who is the bank you make your payments to, and who is the investor?
- How many loans are on the property?
- How many properties do you own?
- What is your household income?
- Has your income fluctuated in the last two years?
- How much money do you have in the bank?
- What are your monthly obligations? (i.e., credit cards, auto loans, living expenses, utilities, other mortgages, medical bills, etc.)
- Has your employment been steady in recent years?

- What are your future plans? (Will you outgrow the property? Do you eventually want to relocate? Will you want to downsize to a smaller property in the coming years?)
- Any significant life changes since you purchased the property?

The answers to these questions will dictate the expectations a homeowner should have. If you as a homeowner are talking to someone who does not ask these questions or cannot accurately set an expectation with you from the onset, then you should really consider finding someone else who can. In my opinion, the expectations of homeowners getting started in this process are critical if indeed they want to minimize any miscommunication, reduce frustrations and stress, avoid surprises, and reach their desired outcome. Any experienced professional will ask these questions and adjust your expectations based on the details of your situation.

As a homeowner you also want to make sure you are clear on certain details so that you do not second-guess a decision. The people you are working with should be able to answer the following questions up front so that you are properly informed from the beginning. If they cannot, you may want to find someone else with more experience to help you handle your short sale.

- What type of credit hit will I take because of a short sale?
- Do I have to be delinquent on payments to get the short sale approved?
- Can my bank pursue me personally (here in my state) if I complete a short sale or foreclose on the property?
- How many short sales have you handled and successfully closed?
- Are you familiar with my bank?
- Do you know who the investor is who owns my mortgage?
- How long does it take for my bank to review short sale requests and issue an approval?
- Is my income or asset situation going to pose an issue on a short sale? If so what can we possible do in order to minimize my potential exposure?
- Will I get a seller incentive or relocation assistance from the bank?
- Will the bank want a cash contribution or promissory note from me?
- Will I have a tax liability associated with the short sale?

When going through a short sale, you need to have realistic expectations in order to avoid surprises. The last thing you want to do as a homeowner or real estate agent is deal with additional frustrations that come with people expecting an approval in thirty days when the reality is that most banks take much longer than that. If you are a real estate agent, do not be optimistic with the expectations you set; instead, be brutally honest. If the homeowners have a loan with a bank that has routinely been slow on previous transactions, for instance, then the homeowners' expectations should be that the transaction will take five to six months. Sometimes "it is what it is", and everyone needs to understand that that up front.

Many homeowners have read and heard about the banks actually giving homeowners money at the closing of a short sale. I have seen a bank give as much as $35,000 to a homeowner at the closing of a short sale. Although this does happen on occasion, you have to remember that every situation is unique and will have a different outcome. When the bank offers the seller an incentive or money at closing, it is normally $1,000 to $3,000. This could be because the homeowner qualified for a particular program, but, realistically a seller incentive should not be expected. The reality is that the seller has received some type of incentive (money given to them by the bank) on roughly 30 percent of the short sales my company has negotiated. On another 30 percent of our short sales, the banks have required that the homeowner actually bring money to closing as a contribution toward the loss being taken by the bank. Yes, this is just as likely to happen as the seller incentive. Setting the right expectation from the onset is critical in order to avoid unhappy clients.

Banks are trying to offset their losses is by requiring homeowners to sign a promissory note as terms of the short sale approval. The promissory note will outline that the seller will repay a portion of the loss over a fixed time frame after the transaction closes. Promissory notes were very popular a few years back and have now been coming up much more often in recent months. In many instances, promissory notes were happening when the loan being short sold was a conventional loan that had mortgage insurance, not the FHA or VA loans. As terms of the approval, the homeowner is required to sign a promissory note, which needs to be paid back over a certain time frame. Promissory notes are typically two to five years and at 0 percent interest. The amount being repaid within a promissory note is in most cases 8 to 15 percent of the total amount lost on the loan and is always negotiable. Banks usually ask for 30 to 60 percent of the loss, but getting them down to 8 to 15 percent is normally doable depending on the financial situation of the homeowner. Obviously every situation is different, but, if the homeowner has a job and the ability to retain the property, it makes more sense to simply get rid of the debt and honor a small promissory note than allow an underwater property to bleed you to death financially.

The buyer and the buyer's real estate agent both need realistic expectations if everyone is going to work together toward getting the short sale transaction approved and closed. If the seller has a loan or loans with certain banks that are routinely slow in reviewing short sale packages, then letting the buyer know that the process is going to take longer than normal is a good idea on the part of the real estate agent. I would rather give the buyer the heads-up than have them get impatient throughout the process and back out of the transaction, leaving the seller back at square one trying to secure another buyer.

I would also discuss with the buyer what their response would be to increase the offer price if the bank does counter it. If they are not willing to increase and the offer is, in your opinion lower than fair market value, then you may be doing your client a disservice by accepting it. You may be better off leaving the property on the market and finding a more sensible buyer with a higher probability of closing. I have been shocked by what some of these buyers' agents tell their buyers and the expectations they set. They are setting the buyer up to get frustrated and inevitably back out of the transaction altogether, which wastes time for everyone involved. This needs to change if we are all going to all work toward getting short sales closed. If you are a real estate professional and you cannot set the proper expectations with both the seller and buyer, you are setting yourself up for inevitable failure and a waste of a lot of time. In order to set these transactions up for success, it is important that you are staying in touch with your market and ensure everyone is clear on what to expect from the onset. If you are a homeowner and are working with an agent who does not know how to set an expectation, then you should consider finding new representation.

Properly Preparing a Short Sale Package

When you have chosen the direction of a short sale and have secured a buyer, the next critical step is preparing the short sale package properly. If you prepare the short sale package the right way from day one, you are positioning your file to go through the process in a much more streamlined manner and avoiding the many frustrations that arise from submitting an incomplete package. If you prepare a file that is incomplete or wrong, then you are setting your transaction up from the onset to be a nightmare, and it is you who is responsible for the headaches that will inevitably pop up.

Many real estate agents, title companies, and attorneys have been taking the "throw everything against the wall and see what sticks" approach to short sales—and that does not work. In a short sale, you need to know how to properly prepare your file prior to submitting it to the bank(s). You need to understand the different scenarios of income and what the banks require to verify each type. If you are not familiar with financial documents, you should not be trying to deal with a banking issue that will require a financial skill set. Doing so would only reduce the likelihood of getting the transaction closed.

Most banks have a short sale package that they require to be completed by the seller and a specific set of documents that will also need to accompany it. The documents usually include the following: most recent 2 years' worth of Tax Returns, most recent 2 months' worth of bank statements, (self-employed would require 6 months of business bank statements) most recent 30 days' worth of pay stubs, (self-employed would be a year to date profit and loss statement from the business) the executed purchase agreement with all addendums and disclosures and an estimated HUD-1 based on the offer and the specific subject property.

Avoiding Multiple Lines of Communication

As a homeowner it is your responsibility to educate yourself as to what options you have and to identify the right direction for you. The problem is that it is nearly impossible to know what options you have, based on the details of your unique situation without having experience.

Therefore, you need to find someone who can explain your options based on experience in dealing with similar scenarios. This is actually a hard thing to accomplish, since very few people have the ability to accurately break down each and every option.

Once you decide on a direction, it is your responsibility to choose the right team of professionals to help you navigate through the process. You have to trust them implicitly to do what they were hired to do and must avoid getting involved more than what is actually needed. If the homeowner—or anyone else for that matter—is communicating with the bank at the same time another third party is also communicating with the bank on the same transaction, you are setting yourself up to fail. Having multiple lines of communication with the bank on a short sale is a recipe for disaster. You will both get contradicting information, which will snowball into other issues that could easily have been avoided if you simply had one person handling the communication with the bank from the onset. Even though you may be trying to help, it is really working against you to get involved in something you are not familiar with. This is another reason why it is important to choose the right team to work with and to allow them to do what you hired them to do.

Evolution of Short Sales Today

As the demand for short sales has increased, we have seen many new companies enter the market. Attorneys saw a niche and felt there was a need by homeowners who needed someone to handle the negotiations with the banks. They obviously had not been handling financing issues and had a learning curve, just like everyone else who got involved in short sales. The reality is that attorneys are not able to do anything different from anyone else handling short sales, as the banks and the investors who own these loans have specific processes in place that each file needs to go through regardless of who is handling the processing/negotiations. I emphasis again that experience is what matters most when it comes to getting your short sale closed. If it is a real estate agent, Title Company, attorney or third party negotiator - the one who has the most experience will secure the best outcome much more often.

I see a benefit to getting information from an attorney, but short sales seldom require any legal action and do not require an attorney to handle them. If homeowners feel more comfortable or protected by having an attorney handle their short sale transactions then they should hire one but should still make sure the attorney has enough experience to get them to the desired outcome. Very few attorneys have experience in this arena or the skill set to successfully navigate through the short sale process with the different banks. Although many of them have jumped into this industry, they are typically trying to learn on the fly and have not successfully closed on enough transactions to garner the necessary experience. A large percentage of them here in Las Vegas have already exited the market once they learned the amount of work that goes into each transaction. Many of the others who continue to handle these transactions charge exorbitant fees in order to cover the employee overhead and still be profitable considering the enormous amount of time it takes to get these short sales closed.

Some of the states most significantly affected by the real estate crash have established new licensing requirements specifically tailored for people who help homeowners through loan modifications and negotiating short sales. Here in Nevada this license requires a finance/banking background so that the people trying to help homeowners actually have the specific skill set and background to properly manage these short sale transactions. Keep in mind that Nevada is a recourse state, which means that banks can sue the homeowner personally for the deficiency. It is crucial for homeowners in Nevada to have the best team available to assist with short sale transactions because the deficiencies can be immense due to the steep decline of property values in that market. The license was initially intended to implement business standards that had to be met by those providing these services. The issue prior to the licensing requirements was that many unscrupulous "loan modification" companies were charging large up-front fees and then never doing anything to help these distressed homeowners. When the license first came out here in Nevada, the number of companies grew quickly, but as these companies have been audited, this number has decreased significantly. The third-party service providers who only specialize in the dealings with the bank for short sale transactions do charge fees for the services they provide, but the companies who are still around should bring to the table a benefit that far exceeds the fee they charge.

What you as a homeowner need to decide is if indeed you feel more comfortable with someone who has a specific license and skill set handling the short sale for you and negotiating the most beneficial terms for you, or if you want a free service from someone that may not be as experienced in handling these transactions. If the likelihood of you actually getting to the desired outcome with the most beneficial terms for you is increased by having a specialist involved, then any additional fee is well worth it. Again you need to educate yourself and make a decision on whom to work with based on their experience in order to put your transaction in the best possible position to get approved and closed.

Besides the attorneys and third-party service providers, another group also moved into the short sale negotiation industry in an attempt to capture market share in a business they were already involved with. These are the title companies that have historically been involved with real estate transactions and have now set up short sale processing/negotiation departments. Title companies are struggling to retain market share which has suffered due to the downturn in the market. In an attempt to stay alive, many have taken on the additional responsibility of negotiating short sales. This may be outside the scope of what they are legally allowed to do in each jurisdiction, but many title companies have jumped into this market with both feet.

Since the title company is supposed to be a neutral third party, I do see somewhat of a conflict of interest. Since they are essentially negotiating the terms of the transaction for the buyer and the seller, being neutral may be difficult. They are really trying to offer a service so that real estate agents send them new escrow business. Since they market short sale processing/negotiations as a free service, they are able to capitalize on getting a high number of escrows. However, the conversation of those short sale negotiations into actual closings is still questionable. As time passes, it will be interesting to see how many lawsuits get filed against these title companies who offer a service that may be considered to be outside of their scope of allowed services. Being a neutral third party also seems to be questionable. All it will take is for one mismanaged file or disgruntled homeowner to complain for these questions to be brought to the surface and then we will see what they can and con not do as it pertains to these transactions.

As a homeowner you have to look at what you get for this free service and then must decide if it is worth it to have them handle your short sale, or if you instead want to have someone else handle it who may be able to secure better terms for you. Are you confident that a title company is motivated by getting you as the seller the best terms, or do you think they are more concerned with getting the transaction closed? If you think they are more concerned with getting the transaction closed, then you have to question whether they are truly negotiating in your best interest. Title companies have been reluctant to issue conversion rate numbers on short sale transactions, so I can only base my opinion on what I have heard—which has been predominantly negative. These negatives typically revolve around the title companies' inability to get transactions closed and getting approvals that incorporate higher than normal contributions to the bank from sellers. In turn, sellers are reluctant to move forward and the transaction fails to close.

Banks are also evolving and some have determined that the best way to process these submissions for short sales is to outsource them to third parties. This is a huge step that many banks are reluctant to take, but the banks who do outsource their short sale transactions should be minimizing costs and increasing production. Why set up a new department and take on the additional costs of training employees if you can have someone step in and take on that responsibility? Some third party companies are already experienced and have systems in place?

Some of these third-party service providers are good and some still lack efficiency, but the overall direction does make sense. Many companies are trying to fill this space but the learning curve associated with it still causes problems. One specific third-party service provider comes to mind when thinking of the problems that arise when companies get in over their heads when they enter a new industry. This company is also a good example of how these third parties are rarely held accountable for errors being made or meeting specific service standards. This specific provider and others are causing serious frustrations and delays due to their internal inefficiency. Why they have chosen to veer off from doing what they have done in the past (helping people with relocation needs) is unknown, but the problems that come up when dealing with them are things that should not still be happening at this stage of the game and really are negatively impacting the whole transaction. If we are going to get through the current problems we are facing someone needs to be held accountable and fix these issues at the third party companies. This is especially troublesome when you consider that the cost of mismanagement is a foreclosure for their customer – that is a mighty price to pay for incompetence.

This is a prime example of how on the surface, things seem to be easy, but when these providers actually enter the industry, they realize how inadequately prepared they really were. This is also a prime example of how no one is held accountable for the internal errors made at the banks and the third-party companies they use, which needs to change. In the big picture, these third-party service providers are a positive addition to the short sale industry as they may enable more transactions to close efficiently. As the investors who own these mortgages and banks establish more standards, these third-party providers should bring to the table even more of a benefit.

Banks Incorporating New Systems

One of the biggest advancements that some banks have made in the last year has been the incorporation of new systems that helped to reduce many of the internal problems they had. The new systems made the short sale review process a much more automated, streamlined process. The frustrations of documents being misplaced or lost altogether have been reduced as a result of these new systems. Imagine submitting documents to the bank, confirming that the documents you sent in have been received, and then a few days later having someone else at the same bank tell you that the documents were missing or were never received. My staff and I still encounter issues with the document upload turnaround times and compliance review, but getting documents over to the banks and confirming that they are received is much better today than it was in the past.

Communication throughout the process was one of the most frustrating things in the short sale approval process. The banks would routinely call the assigned person handling the transaction for the consumer. If that person was unavailable or in the field, then it seemed like everything would be placed on hold until that person touched base with them. When the person handling the file for the homeowner would call back, they would never be able to reach the right person and nothing seemed to get done. The constant phone tag between the banks and the sellers' representatives was another huge communication issue plaguing the industry, but these new systems help to cut those frustrations down. Communication is still at times a huge hurdle; however, with some of the banks' new systems, a lot of the prior communication issues are handled through the systems, which helps to avoid unnecessary delays. Of course this is when the banks have properly trained their staff on how to actually use the system.

Remember that not all banks have incorporated new systems; therefore, misplaced documents and communication hurdles are still encountered often. As new systems are incorporated, it takes many months for each specific bank to adapt to its new system and train its staff as to how the new system works. At my company, we have noticed that in the initial transitioning period, the process actually gets significantly worse for a few months before it becomes more efficient. As such, avoiding a new system in its infancy is in a homeowner's best interest if indeed the homeowner wants to circumvent delays. The key point here is that more and more banks are taking steps to minimize both the misplacing of documents and communication breakdowns throughout the short sale review process. In order to further expedite these transactions, the systems need to also continue to evolve so that a few other extremely time consuming processes are changed.

Changing Buyers

When a short sale has been going through the normal process of being reviewed, the main two objectives seem to be the homeowners' circumstances and the property's current condition/value. Even though the buyer is not the one being reviewed for the short sale approval, most banks refuse to allow the changing of a buyer and therefore keep the seller from moving forward on the same path towards closing. This happens quite often where a potential buyer decides they do not want to buy the property for a variety of reasons and a new buyer must be secured.

Why should that force the whole process to start over from the beginning? It seems that this is an unneeded waste of resources at the bank and could easily be fixed. As long as everything in the file is still up to date and the new offer is in line with the fair market value of the home, I don't understand why the banks refuse to make swapping out a buyer an easier process. Unfortunately, this is precisely the type of thing that makes the banks look as if they are trying to be difficult to work with and also a significant cause for delays in the process. If the buyer is really that important, then it would make sense to do a buyer review, but that should easily be accomplished without needing to start the whole process over again from the start.

Value Discrepancy Issues

On all short sales, the bank wants to make sure they are getting the fair market value for these properties so that they can minimize the losses they are taking. That is understandable; however, it is interesting that some of these investors (predominantly Fannie Mae and Freddie Mac) are trying to force buyers to pay ten to twenty percent more for a home than it is actually worth. Taking steps to minimize losses is good business, but attempting to force buyers to pay more for a home than it is truly worth is unreasonable. These banks/investors are in essence putting hardworking homeowners, who are trying to address the problem, at risk of being foreclosed upon, and that is unjust. They have recently been taking the indefensible stance that they want buyers to pay more for the property than it is worth and if the buyer refuses to pay the inflated price then the bank will just foreclose on these homeowners.

These tactics have been going on for some time now, and someone needs to put a stop to it. All it is doing is causing buyers to back out while also frustrating homeowners to the point where they are disgruntled and no longer want to cooperate with moving forward with a short sale. These homeowners are already losing their homes and the money they have put into their homes over the years while they owned them. They are not getting bailed out by the government like the banks did, and all that money they have lost will never be paid back to them.

Now, even after they are trying to do the right thing (as opposed to just walking away and forcing the bank to foreclose), the banks are blowing the transaction up by making unreasonable purchase price demands on buyers. When this happens, they force everyone to go through the long, drawn-out process of a value dispute and run the risk of losing buyers while also losing the cooperation of these sellers, who have now lost confidence that the bank will work with them on a short sale. This does absolutely nothing beneficial for anyone within the transaction and routinely ends with the home being foreclosed on and another person feeling as if they have been victimized by the banks. In the rare instances a buyer is willing to pay more for the home; it is typically not a family looking to move into the property but more likely an investor who had the money to pay over and above the amount of the appraisal. This means that these tactics are working against American families who are buying homes with the intentions of living in them and just increasing the number of investors who own these homes as rentals. It is extremely frustrating to see this happening but it is the reality of the current environment and is yet another predatory tactic being used by these banks/investors.

Approval Letter Extensions

Another issue that is encountered often, and really makes no sense, actually happens after the short sale has been approved when all of the obstacles should be behind everyone. After a homeowner has cooperated with the bank and gone through the whole process of attaining the approvals to close on a short sale, many times the buyer's financing is delayed. Loans are not as quick in today's market and everything needs to be verified and re-verified in order to close. Thus the process of obtaining a mortgage loan is not what it once was. In today's market, when a buyer needs to secure an FHA or VA loan, it may take thirty to sixty days.

The problem with that is when issuing short sale approval letters, these banks regularly only give the buyer twenty to thirty days to close, and then, when the buyer's loan is not ready, they don't just efficiently issue extensions but instead make the parties involved jump through more hoops to get an extension to the approval letter. Why banks don't just issue approvals granting sixty days to close as a standard makes no sense at all. If they would, then everyone could avoid the additional stress associated with trying to get an extension to close last minute. This is a small thing, but realistically, implementing a small change would go a long way in showing consumers that the banks are not intentionally trying to put homeowners in a bad position.

Some banks are issuing approvals with short time frames to close so that if the transaction does not close in time, they charge the homeowner or the buyer additional fees for an extension. Again this shows how the banks are doing things without thinking and are sometimes operating inefficiently without considering the best interests of all parties involved. As a result the perception has formed that the banks are not working in good faith to help people, but instead are trying to again take advantage of the consumer every chance they get.

Issues that Routinely Get in the Way of Closing

Many different factors have led to seemingly endless frustrations that occur on short sale transactions. Throughout the process of securing an approval and even after the banks have issued approval letters, many things can still cause a transaction to fall apart. This was a huge problem when short sales first started plaguing real estate markets throughout the country and it continues to happen today. People trying to get the transactions approved and closed need time to familiarize themselves with all the moving pieces associated with closing a short sale and the different scenarios that tend to come into play. Based on the reality that every homeowner's situation is unique and every bank and/or investor has a different process one must go through, there was a learning curve on the part of all parties if indeed they were going to properly navigate through the process to cross the finish line. Below are just a few of the issues that routinely get in the way of a short sale closing:

- Lack of communication
- Seller or buyer expectations
- Value discrepancies
- Other liens on the property (i.e. tax liens, judgments, HOA liens, etc.)
- Sellers being required to give contributions unexpectedly and then backing out of the transaction

- Loans being transferred to new servicers in the middle of a short sale
- Banks deciding to foreclose on a property in the middle of a short sale due to lack of communication between the banks and the third party handling the foreclosure
- Losing buyers unexpectedly
- Buyers being unable to secure the loan they need to close
- Senior and junior lien holders not agreeing to the terms
- Buyers' loans not closing in time resulting in the expiration if the short sale approvals
- Mortgage insurance companies being unreasonable with their demands
- Allowing frustrations throughout the process to make you lose focus of the goal

Updated HAFA Guidelines

Ever since the HAFA program came out, revisions have been made but many things have still not been addressed or corrected that will need to be if the program is going to have the positive affect that the government initially expected. The government has been working to refine the HAFA short sale program to make it more efficient so that the process produces more benefits for homeowners, as opposed to just making it more difficult and time consuming. Typically when a new program comes out or new rules are implemented, it will take months before any real progress is made, but at least they have accepted the fact that the program needs to be changed. Identifying issues with the program and taking steps to correct those issues at least demonstrates that they are trying to enhance the productivity of the program. The main changes to HAFA being implemented in early 2013 will revolve around the following three areas:

1. Reducing the paperwork that needs to be completed and making it so every bank is using the same forms, as opposed to each homeowner needing to fill out multiple packets that all basically have the same information in them.

2. Reducing the time banks have to review packets so that a homeowner can get quicker responses. Under the current rules the banks have forty-five days to review submitted packages, but that is not a time frame that is being met in the majority of cases. The new guidelines will give the banks thirty days to review submissions. We don't know if the banks will now be held accountable for their lack of performance, but, based on how bad they have been over the last five years, I would hope someone is taking notice and being held accountable. If anything, the tax payer dollars that went to bail the banks out should have enabled them to incorporate competent management to oversee these programs being rolled out.

3. Allowing more money to go toward junior lien holders. They were initially only allowing $3,000, but obviously that was not reasonable in many cases. The new revisions will allow up to 10 percent of the unpaid principal balance or a maximum amount of $8,500 to go toward junior liens, so that they are more likely to participate with the program.

CHAPTER 6

Fixing the Problem

When trying to identify how exactly to address this problem, there is no simple answer. The solution seems to have as many moving pieces as what it took for the boom to happen to begin with, and as the problem has grown from involving certain pockets of the United States to being a national crisis, the process of fixing it has become that much more complex. The reality is that the problem is going to be difficult to address on a large scale and will require a joint effort by the different investors and banks.

Since many factors played a role in getting us into this situation, trying to get through it is also going to take a combination of different pieces all working together. This is not limited to the investors and banks but also includes the government, real estate professionals, loan officers, developers, and even homeowners all doing their parts. Everyone needs to jointly acknowledge the mistakes made in the past and then take steps to make significant changes to help us get back to the point where our markets are seeing the healthy, modest appreciation numbers that were customary prior to the boom. Below is a breakdown of simple changes each party can implement to start working toward fixing the current problem they all helped create:

Banks and the Government

I'm focusing on banks and the government together due to the fact that the banks are working with the government and taking some guidance from the government in order to help the situation. Both the banks and the government need to start addressing the problem by putting an end to all the misleading information they put out in the media. By misleading consumers with hopes of programs that will help them but then only offering minimal relief, the banks and government are only compounding the problem.

Homeowners will inevitably get more disgruntled after months of paying a trial payment plan on a modification or being told that a short sale approval was on the way only to finally find out that what they had been hoping for is not going to happen. That slap in the face will only enhance the overall public sentiment of distrusting the banks. These types of tactics have been going on for some time, but they don't do anything to help the problem or portray to the average homeowner that the banks are willing to work with them to get through the current hardships they may be facing.

Together, the banks and government also need to come up with and enforce standards to ensure everyone is playing by the same set of rules and so the process of relief can be more streamlined for homeowners trying to do the right thing in addressing the problem. The different banks and servicing companies need to have clear service standards and be held accountable when they internally mismanage a file or misplace documents that have been received. Over the last few years, it is apparent that holding the banks responsible has not been the case. No one seems to be held accountable for errors, and that is one of the biggest problems everyone working on these transactions has in dealing with these banks. However, we cannot focus on the frustrations of the past but will instead hopefully move forward toward a more standardized process for everyone, and that starts with the banks and government.

In setting up standards, one of the critical pieces should be that the bank or servicing company will only communicate directly with the assigned person authorized on the account. No longer should they call the homeowner directly trying to scare them into making a payment. Instead the standards should allow for the enlisted professional to help navigate the transaction toward a successful outcome. Those direct calls from the banks or servicing companies to the homeowner only convolute things and do nothing but portray to the homeowner that the bank is trying to take advantage of them through deceptive practices.

These standards also need to ensure that the banks and servicing companies have the ability to handle every scenario on an individual basis and open up different options based on the details of each predicament. If the necessary relief for the homeowner means that it makes financial sense to reduce the principal balance owed to -110 percent of the current fair market value, then they need to be open to that as an option, especially in areas that have experienced higher depreciation. However, these options must not include extending the loan terms or any other creative way to capitalize on homeowners in the future. Instead the new loan terms need to be beneficial and should not incorporate any hidden agenda on the part of banks to get more money from the homeowners in the future. The banks should never tell the homeowners that they are approved when they still have to go through a trial period on a modification and avoid misleading them into thinking they received principal reductions when in reality they have only provided principal curtailment.

Most homeowners want to stay in their homes, but those who owe significantly more on their home than it is worth see it as a losing proposition financially. These are hardworking people who need a small bailout, just like the banks and many other industries have been getting in recent years. When homeowners occupy the property and want to retain their home, banks should be more willing to work with them to make that happen through true principal reductions. If they are not going to grant a principal reduction or other terms without hidden predatory clauses, then the banks need to be honest and tell the homeowners that they will not work with them and advise them that a short sale is the chosen direction based on their situation. As a result of this small adjustment, the banks would again gain confidence from the consumers and take a smaller loss on these toxic mortgages. In turn the rate of foreclosures would go down, inventory of bank owned homes would decrease and home values would be that much closer to stabilizing on a larger level.

Banks need to understand that many homeowners are encountering something they are not familiar with and certainly never intended to deal with. A heightened element of stress goes along with that lack of familiarity with the whole situation. By making the process of both loan modifications and short sales more standardized, banks can enable homeowners to address the problem in a more streamlined manner so they can get this stressful situation behind them quicker. Most homeowners at this point don't trust that the banks are doing anything in their best interest and believe that the banks are only trying to deceive them with hidden future exposure. This needs to change.

After years of hearing the many horror stories about banks, many homeowners have in turn formed the opinion that the banks are always out to wrong them. Homeowners have come to my team with stories of banks approving loan modifications and then backing out after the fact, approving short sales only to turn around and file a lawsuit against the homeowner for the loss, trying to force a buyer to pay more for a home than it is truly worth, or saying that they are working toward a short sale only to then foreclose on the property in the middle of the process. By implementing certain changes, we can acknowledge that these problems have existed but can then start to positively reinforce to homeowners that banks are implementing changes to minimize these things from happening in the future. We need to acknowledge what the real current property value is and accept that as the price as opposed to what has recently been taking place with Fannie Mae and Freddie Mac. This will help rebuild consumer confidence as opposed to working in the opposite direction. They need to show that they are helping to offer homeowners a true element of relief.

Steps Banks, Investors and the Government Can Take to Begin Fixing the Problem:

- Offer seller incentives so that homeowners are motivated to work with the bank, as opposed to the alternative.
- Be accountable when someone internally drops the ball on a transaction and also implement an escalation process to efficiently fix the problem when this does happen.
- Continue to evolve with the market and train your staff so that when you see a reoccurring issue on these transactions you can fix it.

- Allow buyers to rent properties back to the current homeowner after taking over ownership of the property, as long as they are not blood relatives and do not have any other relationship other than owner/tenant. A buyer who is buying a home as an investment has every right to rent the home back to the previous owner when that will increase their return on that investment. As long as the bank is getting a fair market purchase price for the property why do they care if the seller wants to rent the property back?
- Address value discrepancies in a more reasonable manner and cease practices that include trying to force buyers to overpay for a property. (For more information, refer to the lender section regarding the HomePath program.)
- Properly train employees prior to trusting them to handle these types of transactions.
- Continue to work together to revise guidelines as needed in an environment that is constantly changing.
- Rebuild consumer confidence, i.e., reassure them that you are trying to help them through actions as opposed to making false promises.

Real Estate Agents

Real estate agents are going to play a critical role in moving these communities forward toward getting back to normal. As a real estate agent, you cannot avoid these types of transactions but instead have to educate yourself and possibly align yourself with a third party that knows exactly how these transactions work. This will help you proactively secure new business. By embracing your market and securing new business, you are also putting yourself in a position to positively impact the same clients that you may have initially helped during the boom. You shouldn't feel as if you are responsible for the scenario they are now in, but instead help them by addressing the current problem. In turn you will increase your ability to generate income at the same time. Without the efforts of real estate professionals, these markets will continue to struggle and it will take much longer for them to stabilize. Make an effort to educate homeowners and accurately advise them on what options they truly have so that they are in a position to make a decision on how to address their individual problem.

As real estate agents, you cannot be stuck in the old way of doing business but instead need to evolve with the market. In doing this you will gain more referral sources and clientele. It is not your fault that the collapse happened, but it is your responsibility to help educate homeowners and identify the best way to help them out of a bad situation. Maybe you have the experience it takes to navigate the process on their behalf, but maybe it is best to enlist a third party who may have more experience, which in turn will increase the likelihood of getting your client the desired outcome. The more clients you help, the more income you will generate and the more future business you will capture as the market inevitably changes again.

Over the last five years, we have seen dramatic changes in the mindset of many real estate agents. Some high-producing agents of the past were not taking any short sale listings based on the fact that they lacked familiarity with these types of transactions. In many cases they also felt as if their past clients who they had helped purchase the home would in some way hold that against them, as if they had anything to do with the collapse. Others were taking them on, but the tedious process was frustrating them, as was the fact that they were only closing on a small percentage of them. One agent had never done a short sale and avoided them like the plague until we met and he worked with us in preparing a homeowner (joint client) for the process. After that he was more confident taking on short sale listings and trusting us to do our part. He attracts new clients and then sends them to us to take care of all the dealings with the bank. All while he continues to build his pipeline of future business. Fast-forward from when we first met to today and that same real estate agent has a continuous pipeline of ten-plus short sale closings on a monthly basis and in turn his business has grown while being in what was considered a bad market.

Without the joint efforts of real estate professionals and the assistance of experienced third parties helping to educate and navigate through these transactions, the existing problem will continue to linger for an extended period of time. This is avoidable if we can help homeowners understand the benefits of moving forward and addressing the problem. As these toxic loans are modified or short sold, the different markets will slowly stabilize. Eventually, we will get back to the traditional ways of doing real estate. Until that takes place, the real estate agents who embrace the current environment and see it as an opportunity to build future business will have a huge advantage over those who choose to avoid these transactions due to their inability to adapt or because of their fear of the challenges that come along with them.

Steps Real Estate Agents Can Take to Begin Fixing the Problem:

- Educate homeowners.
- Identify whether you have the ability, experience, and time to navigate to the finish line or if you should instead enlist a third party.
- Never allow the numerous hurdles you will encounter to cause you to lose sight of the goal.
- Don't be scared to fail, but instead take on the challenges you face in your market.
- Set an expectation with your clients so that you are positioned to be successful.
- Many things are out of your control. It is your job to identify solutions to problems as they surface so your clients can obtain the outcomes they desire.

Homeowners

As a homeowner it is your responsibility to do your part if we are going to move forward and get through the current real estate issues we are all facing. Once you realize that you are in a situation that needs to be addressed, be proactive and educate yourself as to what options you have. The simple fact that you are reading this book says that you are already educating yourself and have acknowledged a problem exists. Expecting the problem to fix itself is not going to get you any closer to being in a sustainable long-term situation. Obviously everyone has a different set of circumstances, but based on your scenario, you need to understand what the problem really is and what options you have so that you can move forward addressing your particular situation in the best possible way to secure a long-term solution. The worst thing you can do is nothing, but unfortunately that is what many people have been doing—which only delays the inevitable and actually prolongs the problem within their communities.

Once you identify the best direction based on your situation, your next step is to align yourself with the right team of professionals so that they can help navigate your transaction toward the desired outcome. This does not mean you have a 100 percent guarantee of getting to that outcome, but by having the most knowledgeable people working on your behalf, you are putting yourself in position to have the highest probability of getting there. Although many companies have experience at this point the reality is that no one converts on 100 percent of short sale transactions. It is flat out impossible to close on every transaction due to the fact that each one has so many different variables.

As you go through the process, you will encounter issues and you will need to work with your chosen professionals as a team to get through those hurdles while always staying focused on the goal of a successful transaction. Never allow problems that are out of your control to snowball into bigger issues; instead, find a solution to whatever the problem may be while always staying focused on the goal.

This situation is not about pride of ownership but instead is about making an important financial decision that makes the most sense for you and your family long term. You need to step back and look at your house as an investment that has gone wrong or a business that needs to make dramatic changes in order to stay profitable—and make the right business decision accordingly. The one thing that we should have all learned over the last few years, as we have gone through the boom and into the current collapse, is that we never know what is going to happen in the future. Based on that reality, we need to make difficult decisions today, knowing that they could impact our family's financial livelihood in the years to come. We cannot allow emotional ties, negative credit marks or anything else impact decisions that may have long-term repercussions and we cannot take things for granted, as we never know what may be around the corner as we go through our lives. We can lose our jobs. We can be forced to relocate. We may outgrow our homes as neighborhoods deteriorate. We may encounter health issues, and the last thing anyone wants is to look back wishing they had the money they threw away on a negative-equity property when it is too late.

Builders and Developers

Builders and developers cannot go back to fix any of the problems they helped create, but they can acknowledge the mistakes they made in the past so that we can all avoid those same issues from resurfacing. They have to develop new communities, of course, but they need to build homes knowing the true value of the finished product and then build in profit margins based on their market. They cannot simply build homes without making sure they are offering a good product and they must know what the value of these homes should be when they are completed in order to build in a reasonable profit margin. By offering a good product at the going rate, they can still sell homes while providing the consumer with the home they desire.

They also need to control the number of new homes they are building while we try to stabilize these markets and avoid having an abundance of inventory based on the demand in the area. Building at an overly aggressive pace would be counterproductive and may actually end up compounding the issue. In order to stabilize the market and get back to where we need to be we need to have a normal inventory of available homes, both new homes and re-sales. The different counties and cities issuing permits will need to take this into consideration in attempt to control how quickly new homes are being built, which will help ensure that a healthy supply-and-demand balance is reached.

Lenders

As a loan officer or mortgage lender, obviously the banks to a certain extent dictate the rules and you are simply given the guidelines to follow. This is going to continue to be the case for years to come, but you still need to learn from the mistakes made during the boom that caused the collapse that inevitably followed.

The banks have rolled out the new HomePath loan program specifically for Fannie Mae and Freddie Mac properties that have been foreclosed upon. The program does not require an appraisal. This seems to be another creative way for the banks/government to control the market through artificially inflating home values with these sales. This program also enables investors to purchase non-owner occupied properties with a minimal down payment. If investors/speculators are again allowed to purchase properties without having any significant skin in the game, doesn't that sound similar to the loans offered during the boom?

The simple fact that Fannie Mae and Freddie Mac are allowing such a program to exist after everything they have gone through is alarming. They are putting themselves in a position to foreclose on homeowners and then go out and re-sell these homes for an inflated amount due to the fact that an appraisal is not required in order to obtain financing. Has the government, along with Fannie Mae and Freddie Mac, not learned a lesson from the problems these types of programs will inevitably cause? This program gives the banks motivation to actually foreclose on homeowners and then go back and take on a loan with a new buyer, who is walking into a negative-equity situation from day one without having any significant amount of their own money at risk.

These same government entities are also trying to use this as a way to force owner occupied buyers to overpay for properties in a short sale. If these buyers will not accept the inflated price or cannot secure the needed financing due to the appraisal requirement to get a conventional loan, then the bank will foreclose and take the appraisal contingency out of the picture. Then they can turn around and sell it for an inflated price to an investor/speculator who intends to rent it out. Fannie and Freddie make more money, put a homeowner who was trying to do the right thing on the streets, and then put more people into a situation where they may make a decision to walk away in the future if the values do not go up as anticipated.

The new program clearly shows that Fannie and Freddie have not learned from the many mistakes of the past. This seems to be a malicious tactic that the government is resorting to in order to capture more money in the short term without any regard for the possible long-term consequences. It has a negative impact on average Americans who are trying to purchase homes for their families, and that is unfortunate. These types of things need to change if indeed we are going to avoid running into similar situations in the future where speculators are able to get overleveraged in real estate all while having very little skin in the game. If the government fails to see the obvious issues pertaining to this program and chooses not to adjust the guidelines, then I fear we may all be in for a long recovery process.

Conclusion

We have all grown up with the mind-set that our home is the safest investment we could ever have and that it will always appreciate in value. In recent years, as the boom turned to the collapse, we have all been forced to step back and reassess whether that is actually true or if things have changed that much from our parents' and grandparents' generations to ours. Homeownership will inevitably revert back to what it was in the past as we get through the current problems, but it is going to take time. Many factors came into play for the boom to happen, and those factors ended up forming the groundwork for the collapse that inevitably followed. The reality is that homeownership should still be part of the American dream and will again be a solid long-term investment for your family.

This recent crisis is not a sign that homeownership is a thing of the past. It is just affirmation that we all collectively need to act more responsibly. The government and the banks need to stop allowing people to obtain loans when their financials show an inability to sustain the payments and must require that these buyers have skin in the game. Homeowners need to avoid the temptation of getting into a property that may be more than what they can truly afford long-term. Once certain changes are made and these markets stabilize, many American families are going to again see homeownership as a safe, long-term investment and realize that homeownership is still something worth working hard to attain.

Glossary of Terms

Appraisal – The true fair market value of a property based on comparable sales in the immediate area over the last 90 days. These sales need to include short sales and foreclosure sales that have taken place in order to accurately depict to the bank the homes true value.

Authorization letter -- A letter from the homeowner, authorizing their lender to discuss personal information with the assigned third party. Letter includes authorized party name and contact information, the property address, loan reference number and the homeowners contact information.

Broker Price Opinion (BPO) – A neutral third party opinion of value for a property that has a mortgage being modified or short sold. (Ordered by the bank being asked to take a loss and therefore BPO evaluations are not always neutral)

Bankruptcy – A proceeding in U.S. District Court wherein debtors who cannot meet the claims of their creditors may be adjudged bankrupt by the court. There are three common types:

> **Chapter 7** - "Debtor Wipeout". The court oversees the liquidation of the debtors' non- exempt assets, distributing the cash proceeds proportionally amongst their creditors.

> **Chapter 11** - This is a business reorganization proceeding.

> **Chapter 13** - "Debtor Workout". This is the almost-automatic choice of most trustors seeking to use a bankruptcy filing to delay the inevitable trustee's sale as long as they can. It's hypothetically possible to drag out a Chapter 13 proceeding for several years. The purpose of this proceeding is to give a "wage

earner" time for rehabilitation, a temporary respite free from the collection efforts of creditors.

Closing/settlement – The final step in the sale of a home where all required documents are signed, funds are disbursed and keys to the home are transferred to the new owner. In some cases, both the buyer and seller (and their representatives) will meet together, perhaps with an attorney or other settlement official (Escrow Company) as required by state law. A "split" closing/settlement can occur in some cases, where the buyer and seller complete document signing in separate locations.

Conforming mortgage – A mortgage loan that meets the lending standards of Fannie Mae and Freddie Mac, the two major entities that buy mortgages on the secondary market, helping ensure that primary lenders having sufficient funding to make new home loans less than $417,000.

Contingency – A legal requirement in a contract, often with a time limit, which must be fulfilled for the contract to remain valid. Buyers often include contingencies related to appraisal of the property, ability to obtain financing, approval of inspection results, obtaining clear title to the property, and so on.

Deed In Lieu of Foreclosure (DIL) – The voluntary surrender of property by an owner/borrower to a lien holder that eliminates the need to continue foreclosure action by the lien holder. The lien holder can refuse to accept the Deed in Lieu and file a Notice of Non Acceptance with the County Recorder.

Defaulted loan – The status of a loan, as determined by the lender, indicating that the borrower has missed making one or more regular payments.

Double Ending a Transaction – When an individual real estate agent works both the listing and buyers sides of a single transaction, enabling them to generate both sides of the overall commission.

Equity – The portion of a home's value that is owned by the homeowner. A homeowner's equity is determined by subtracting the amount of any remaining mortgage(s) owed to lenders from the home's fair market value.

Equity Stripping – When the buyer artificially inflated the purchase price in order to capitalize on the difference in the form of cash back to them from the seller. This also happens when a lender charges excessive fees on a refinance; therefore, reducing the amount of equity the homeowner then has.

Financial worksheet – Spreadsheet that indicates all household income less all household expenses. Often savings and other assets are indicated as well. Documents to support the calculations may be required, such as bank statements, savings accounts, investments, cash, or receipts and invoices / copies of late bills.

Foreclosure – The process through which a lender can sell or repossess (take ownership of) a property in order to recover some of or the entire amount owed on a defaulted loan secured by the property.

Foreclosure Alternative – The process through a loan modification, DIL or a short sale which enables a lender to avoid going through a foreclosure.

Home Affordable Foreclosure Alternative (HAFA) – Government short sale program that many banks are being pressured into utilizing. It is designed to help homeowners address the problem through a short sale but has been changing since its inception in order to actually be the benefit that was anticipated.

Home Affordable Modification Program (HAMP) – Government loan modification program that many banks have been using. It is designed to help homeowners reduce their monthly mortgage payments by reducing the interest rate or extending out the terms of the loan.

Hardship letter – A letter submitted to a lender (as part of a short-sale or loan modification package) indicating the reasons why the borrower can no longer afford to make the current mortgage payments or retain the property.

Investor – The investor is the actual owner of the mortgage behind the scenes who invested in buying the loan. They are in most cases not the company that homeowners make the payment to each month but the ones calling the shots behind the scenes on short sales and other foreclosure alternatives. (Fannie Mae and Freddie Mac are the two largest)

Junior Lien – A lien, usually a mortgage loan, that is behind a Senior Lien. (first mortgage) Lien priority is generally established by order of recordation. NOTE: if you refinance a 1st mortgage on a property with a 2nd mortgage already in place the new 1st mortgage holder will require a subordination agreement from Junior Lien holders to legally establish the new mortgage holder as 1st or Senior Position.

Lender-approved short sale – Conducting a short sale with the lender agreeing to accept the proceeds of the sale and "forgive" the remaining amount of mortgage owed.

Lien – A legal claim on a property whereby the property serves as collateral for a debt or other obligation owed by the property owner to a creditor, service provider, or other entity.

Loan modification – A transaction in which lender agrees to modify any or some of the terms of the mortgage. This is a process where an existing note is modified, but not cancelled. Changes may include: extending the term of the loan, changing the monthly payments, changing the interest rate, etc. Some loan modifications are temporary and others are permanent.

Loan term – The period of time over which a loan must be repaid, e.g., 15, 20, 30 or 40 years.

Loss-mitigation – Home mortgage lenders look to limit losses on delinquent mortgages by working out solutions with borrowers through their Loss Mitigation Departments.

Multiple listing service (MLS) – A database of information on properties for sale that is accessible to all subscribing real estate brokers and their agents.

Non-performing asset – An asset (Mortgage) that does not produce money for the owner. (Meaning that the payments are not being made)

Notice of default (NOD) – An official notice filed and recorded by a designated trustee at the request of a lender indicating lender has commenced foreclosure action.

Pocket Listings – When the listing agent does not put an available home on the market as available to all potential buyers, but instead holds it only for buyers they may bring to the table to purchase the property. This enables them to receive both sides of the commission.

Pre-foreclosure sale – Selling your home before your lender initiates the foreclosure process.

Principal – The amount of money borrowed from a lender (does not include interest owed).

Private Mortgage Insurance (PMI) – A policy of insurance paid for by the borrower to protect the lender in the event the borrower defaults on the mortgage. Typically PMI is required by the mortgage holder when the down payment is less than 20% of the purchase price. (Loan is more than 80% of the current value)

Proceeds – In terms of a home sale, the amount of money left after all other debts and obligations related to the sale have been paid.

Promissory Note – When the bank or Mortgage Insurance Company requires that the homeowner (Seller of a short sale) repays a certain amount of the banks loss over a fixed term. Typically 3-5 years at 0% interest.

Real Estate Owned (REO) – A property owned by a lender after a foreclosure has taken place (also, "bank owned").

Seller contribution – When the bank or Mortgage Insurance Company requires that the homeowner (Seller of a short sale) contributes money towards their loss on the loan. This is based on the homeowners' financial situation and is negotiable in most cases.

Seller Incentive – When the bank actually gives the homeowner (seller on a short sale) money at the closing of the transaction. This is given to them when they qualify for certain short sale programs like HAFA. The incentive is typically given for keeping the property in good condition and cooperating with the bank to avoid a foreclosure as opposed to ignoring the problem. In many instances it is used to offset relocation expenses associated with moving.

Senior Lien – A lien, usually a mortgage loan, that is the first mortgage. Lien priority is generally established by order of recordation and the senior has priority over other liens that may be on the property.

Servicer – A financial institution that manages loans for investors (lenders), including billing, payments, accounting, communications with borrowers, etc. Some investors/lenders act as their own servicers, while most hire outside companies to manage their loan portfolios.

Settlement – When a lender agrees to accept less than the full amount owed on the mortgage. In a short sale the homeowner is not retaining the home but in a second mortgage settlement the bank will accept the settlement of the junior lien and also allow the homeowner to retain the home. In this case the second mortgage being settled would be satisfied and the homeowner would only have the 1st mortgage left.

Short payoff – A lender agrees to accept less than the full balance owed on a loan.

Short sale – The sale of a home in which the lender(s) agrees to accept less than the full amount owed to satisfy the debt allowing the debt to be 'paid off', short of the full balance owed on the loan.

Short-sale package – Forms and instructions provided by a lender to a borrower interested in obtaining the lender's approval for a short sale. Also, the collection of documents – including financial statements, hardship letter, sales contract, etc. – submitted to a lender as a request for short-sale approval.

Straw Buyer – A person acting as the buyer based on their ability to secure the needed loan to purchase a property but really just a front person for the true buyer who is for some reason unable to obtain the needed financing.

Third Party Service Provider – Third party company (Attorney, Title Company, Licensed Company) that is providing services to another party. Third parties are used by homeowners, real estate agents and even banks utilize the services of an outside company.

Toxic Mortgage Portfolio – A group of mortgages that are in default or in a market that has seen significant depreciation. The losses that may be taken on these overleveraged mortgages is unknown and therefore considered to be toxic.

Under water (also, upside down) – When the mortgage loan balance currently owed on a home is greater than the home's current fair market value.

Workout or loan modification – A plan negotiated between a borrower and lender to change the original terms of a loan so that the borrower can afford to continue to make mortgage payments. A workout may involve extending the loan term with smaller payments, a scheduled repayment of missed payments and penalties, reducing the interest rate, refinancing or other approach.

1099-C – IRS Form 1099-c is issued by lenders when they cancel out or forgive debt associated with a mortgage loan. A lender may issue a 1099-c on a short sale, settlement or principal reduction modification. The 1099-c is the tax form used by banks enabling them to write off the loss they took. Depending on the situation the homeowner may have a phantom income tax associated with that amount of debt relief.

> **Note:** The 2007 Mortgage and Debt Relief act was extended through 2013 which grants most homeowners an exemption to the phantom income tax associated with these 1099s. (As long as the loans were used to purchase or upgrade a primary residence)

Examples of Different Options:

Short Pay Refinances:

<u>Example 1:</u>

Homeowner owes 1st mortgage $467,660

Through negotiations with the bank we were successful in achieving the desired outcome which was a short payoff – refinance.

Current Appraised Value $315,000

Amount of the banks issued payoff demand for the refinance

$287,487

Amount of the homeowners' new loan

$305,000

<u>Example 2:</u>

Homeowner owes 1st mortgage $306,400

Homeowner owes 2nd mortgage $75,547

Through negotiations with the bank we were successful in achieving the desired outcome which was a short payoff – refinance on both liens.

Current Appraised Value $267,000

Amount of the banks issued payoff demand for the refinance

Senior Lien $254,950

Junior Lien $1,000

Amount of the homeowners' new loan

$257,655

<u>Example 3:</u>

Homeowner owes 1st mortgage $458,750

Through negotiations with the bank we were successful in securing an approved short payoff demand from the bank.

Current Appraised Value $285,000

Amount of the banks issued payoff demand for the refinance

$279,000

Amount of the homeowners' new loan

$275,000

Loan Modifications:

<u>Example 1:</u>

Homeowner initially owed 1st mortgage $263,928

      Monthly Payment $1,666

Homeowner initially owed 2nd mortgage $32,360

      Monthly Payment $250

Current Appraised Value $215,000

After going through the whole process of submitting the requested financial documents and negotiating for a loan modification we were able to secure the following outcome for our client:

      Homeowner now owes the 1st mortgage $263,928

      New Monthly Payment $863

When negotiating this modification we also negotiated and settled the 2nd mortgage that was owed $75,650 for $1,000 cash. In this scenario that reduced the total monthly expenses for the homeowner by $1,050.

Examples of Different Options

<u>Example 2:</u>

Homeowner initially owed 1st mortgage	$447,886
Monthly Payment	$4,634
Current Appraised Value	$415,000

After going through the whole process of submitting the requested financial documents and negotiating for a loan modification we were able to secure the following outcome for our client:

Homeowner now owes the 1st mortgage	$447,886
New Monthly Payment	$2,233

In this scenario we were able to reduce the total monthly expenses for the homeowner by $2,400.

<u>Example 3:</u>

Homeowner initially owed 1st mortgage	$388,000
Monthly Payment	$3,022
Current Appraised Value	$295,000

After going through the whole process of submitting the requested financial documents and negotiating for a loan modification we were able to secure the following outcome for our client:

Homeowner now owes the 1st mortgage	$260,560
New Monthly Payment	$1,732

When negotiating this modification we were successful in negotiating not just a rate reduction but also principal reduction, reducing the amount owed on the loan by $129,000. On top of that we also reduced the total monthly expense for the homeowner by $1,290.

Junior Lien Settlements:

<u>Example 1:</u>

Homeowner owed 1st mortgage	$284,500
Homeowner owed 2nd mortgage	$75,650
Current Appraised Value	$245,000

After negotiating with the junior lien holder we got them to accept a settlement on the account for a flat $5,000 which also reduced the homeowners' monthly payments by $572.

<u>Example 2:</u>

Homeowner owed 1st mortgage	$351,000
Homeowner owed 2nd mortgage	$91,500
Current Appraised Value	$295,000

After negotiating with the junior lien holder we got them to accept a settlement on the account for a flat $8,100 which also reduced the homeowners' monthly payments by $430.

<u>Example 3:</u>

Homeowner owed 1st mortgage	$225,000
Homeowner owed 2nd mortgage	$72,000
Current Appraised Value	$190,000

After negotiating with the junior lien holder we got them to accept a settlement on the account for a flat $5,000 which also reduced the homeowners' monthly payments by $540.

Short Sales:

Example 1:

Homeowner owed 1st mortgage	$122,816
Homeowner owed 2nd mortgage	$94,227
Current Appraised Value	$140,000
Homeowners Monthly Income	$9,600

Through negotiations with the bank we were able to secure the short sale approval with the following terms.

Payoff to 1st Mortgage	Full Payoff
Seller Contribution	$0
Payoff to the 2nd Mortgage	$6,252
Seller Contribution	$0

As terms of the transaction the bank absorbing the loss on the short sale waived their legal right to pursue the client for the amount of their loss. ($87,975)

Example 2:

Homeowner owed 1st mortgage	$111,000
Current Appraised Value	$50,000
Homeowners Monthly Income	$7,600

Through negotiations with the bank we were able to secure the short sale approval with the following terms.

Payoff to 1st Mortgage	$39,970
Seller Contribution	$0

As terms of the transaction the bank absorbing the loss on the short sale waived their legal right to pursue the client for the amount of their loss. ($71,030)

<u>Example 3:</u>

Homeowner owed 1st mortgage	$188,000
Homeowner owed 2nd mortgage	$47,100
Current Appraised Value	$70,000
Homeowners Monthly Income	$3,700

Through negotiations with the bank we were able to secure the short sale approval with the following terms.

Payoff to 1st Mortgage	$57,698
Seller Incentive **(Paid to seller)**	$3,000

As terms of the transaction the bank absorbing the loss on the short sale waived their legal right to pursue the client for the amount of their loss and also gave the homeowner $3,000 at closing.

Payoff to the 2nd Mortgage	$3,000
Seller Contribution	$0